Beginner's Guide To YouTube
2022 Edition

How To Start & Grow a Successful & Profitable YouTube Channel

Ann Eckhart

Ann Eckhart

BEGINNER'S GUIDE TO YOUTUBE
2022 EDITION

How To Start & Grow a Successful & Profitable YouTube Channel

By Ann Eckhart

TABLE OF CONTENTS

INTRODUCTION

I began my YouTube journey nearly a decade ago about five years after I had quit my corporate job to start a home-based gift basket business. And while sales were strong to start, orders slowed down in the summer, and I needed a way to liquidate inventory.

I decided to give Ebay a shot, only having ever purchased one thing on the site before then. My excess gift basket supplies sold quickly on the site, which led me to test out selling stand-alone gift items such as ceramics, books, and plush. I bought these items from the same wholesale suppliers I was ordering gift basket supplies from, taking a chance that they might sell well enough to fill in during the slow season for gift baskets.

Shockingly, my sales exploded! So much so that by the end of the year, I had ditched the gift baskets in favor of selling gift items. I eventually expanded to selling on Amazon, and my business grew every year.

Until the year it did not. Until the year my sales not only did not grow, but instead started to plummet.

I had been early to the online selling game. When I first started selling on Ebay, Ebay was the only shopping site that allowed third-party sellers. In fact, Ebay was pretty much the only website that sold anything besides books. Amazon, if you are old enough to remember, initially started as an online book store. It took them several years before they started to sell anything other than media.

For those of us who were the first to sell online, there was virtually no competition anywhere on the world wide web. Ebay was not just "the" place to sell; it was the "only" place to sell. Sales came in fast and steady with little effort other than getting a listing up and then shipping it out. My business was, I have to admit, pretty easy to run!

But eventually, the rest of the world caught up to online shopping. Not only were other people starting to sell the same items that I was, but the wholesale companies I bought from were also starting to sell directly to customers online, including setting up shop on both Ebay and Amazon. After years of no competition, I was suddenly surrounded by competitors who were undercutting my prices and offering perks I could not afford, such as free shipping. Seemingly overnight, I could not stay competitive, and my business seemed doomed.

But then I found YouTube. And through YouTube, my business was given a new life. In fact, YouTube saved my business.

I had never watched a YouTube video before that fateful day when I did an internet search about selling on Ebay. I was hoping I would find a book or website that would help me figure out what to do with my business, a magic bullet to help me salvage what I had worked so hard to build.

So, imagine my surprise when my search results revealed several YouTube videos with titles such as "What I sold on Ebay from garage sales" and "How I make money selling used clothing from thrift stores." Intrigued, I followed the links and found a small group of people who called themselves "pickers." These "pickers," or "resellers" as most people now call them, were making videos on YouTube about their thriving Ebay businesses. And not one of them was buying new items wholesale.

I quickly became immersed in the videos these "pickers" were sharing about how they were selling garage sale and thrift store finds on Ebay. While I had always known that there were antique dealers on Ebay, I somehow never made the connection that I, too, could sell secondhand items online. I saw antiques as a specialized skill set, one I knew nothing about. But "antiques" is just the tip of the iceberg when it comes to finding items to resell. And I quickly saw how I, too, could sell used items.

My business, which I had thought was over, suddenly got a new life as I learned all about reselling. While it was hard to give up the ease of ordering new items directly from the manufacture (complete with photos and measurements), I was desperate to avoid having to go back to working for someone else. So, I hunkered down and learned all that I could.

It took a lot of trial and error, but I eventually was successfully able to transition my business away from selling new gift products to selling thrifted finds. I started scouring estate sales for vintage collectibles, and I went to half-off day at the thrift store to buy clothing to resell. My business was saved, and it was thanks to the people who were making videos on YouTube. Those YouTube creators, and the site itself, not only saved my business, but learning how to resell secondhand items eventually led me to writing books such as the one you are currently reading!

When I first started watching YouTube videos, I interacted with the video creators by leaving comments on their uploads and formed friendships that last to this day. They all encouraged me to upload my own videos, but I was terrified. I hated public speaking and being on camera. But eventually, I took the leap and gained the courage to start my own channel.

My first YouTube videos were terrible: I used an old iPhone (I think it was an iPhone 4) and, since I initially filmed in my basement office, the lighting was terrible. But I kept going, slowly gaining confidence in my filming abilities, and growing an audience.

I would gladly give you the URL to my first channel, except for the fact that it no longer exists. Why? Well, because I made a big mistake when I started my first channel, and that was that I did not create it under a Google account, which meant that I could not monetize it. In other words, I was producing videos that were getting a good number of views, but my channel was not making any money.

See, back when I first started on YouTube, you could sign up for a channel using any email address, so I used the one that came with my internet provider. However, you could only monetize your channel if you signed up using a Gmail account, the email that Google provides.

Now, it is essential to know that you can no longer make the mistake I did. Today you must sign up for a YouTube channel with a Google Gmail account. However, back when I started, you could use any email from any provider; and doing this meant I was unable to monetize my content.

After realizing my error, I started a new channel under a Google account and began the long process of rebuilding my audience by urging them to subscribe to my new channel. It took a while to move my audience from my old channel to my new one, but I deleted my original channel and focused on my new channel once I had. To be honest, it was nice to start fresh as I was more comfortable on camera and had upped my production value. But even better was that I started to earn money from my videos. Finally!

After a few years with just one channel, I started a second channel. Why start a second channel when I already had a successful one? Well, it was because I wanted to upload different content. While my first channel focused solely on my Ebay business, I initially started my second channel to focus on my Walt Disney World vacation vlogs. At the time, I anticipated going down to Orlando, Florida, twice a year and filming lots of videos for that channel.

However, life happened, and I became a full-time caregiver for my elderly father. Not only were vacations out of the question, but reselling had to take a backseat as it required too much time and effort. I needed to streamline all my businesses, and that included YouTube. Figuring out what to do took me on a roller coaster of a journey with attempts at various content, and at one point, I almost gave up on YouTube.

But giving up YouTube was harder than sticking with it. After all, I had spent years growing my channels. Eventually, I had to take an "I can only do what I can do" attitude regarding what types of videos I could film and which channel to put them on. At the end of the day, I reminded myself that I started making YouTube videos for fun. Sure, the extra money was nice. But I needed to enjoy myself if I was going to continue producing content.

Today, I still have my two YouTube channels. "Ann Eckhart" has gone from reselling content to subscription box reviews and shopping hauls. And my second channel, which was once titled "SeeAnnAtWDW," is now "Ann Eckhart Vlogs," where I post, you guessed it, vlogs. While I am not currently able to vlog any Disney World vacations, I can vlog my local shopping trips. You would be surprised at how many people love grocery shopping vlogs!

As I said earlier, my YouTube journey has been a roller coaster. There have been times where I was consistently earning over $1,200 a month from my videos, and other times where I had to take a break from filming, which made my earnings plummet. I have changed my content and my upload schedule more times than I can count, and my channels have suffered for it as YouTube favors consistency.

Today, however, I have found a happy medium for my channels. And fortunately for you, you will be learning from all my mistakes, which will help you to be successful right out of the gate.

This book is titled "Beginner's Guide To YouTube," but in fact, it is the ultimate guide to help you not only start a channel but also grow it. From walking you through the process of signing up for your YouTube and Google accounts and monetizing your content to marketing your videos and growing your audience, this book covers it all in a straight-forward, easy-to-follow format.

Whether you have yet to start your YouTube channel or have already started posting videos, I guarantee that this book has something in it to help you succeed and grow!

YOUTUBE STATISTICS

- Founded in February 2005 by three PayPal employees: Chad Hurley, Steve Chen, and Jawed Karim
- By the end of 2005, YouTube was hosting over two million videos per day with an average of 20 million daily active users

- Google purchased YouTube in 2006 for $1.65 billion
- The current CEO is Susan Wojcicki, who was involved in the founding of Google and was Google's first marketing manager in 1999
- YouTube is headquartered in San Bruno, CA, between San Francisco and San Jose next to Interstate 380
- YouTube has 10,000+ employees spread across eight office locations in six countries
- Total number of YouTube active users: 2+ billion (this accounts for almost one-third of the internet)
- Total number of YouTube daily active users: 122 million (62% of these users are in the United States)
- Average time each user spends on YouTube per day: 19.11 minutes (#2 in global internet engagement)
- Total daily hours of YouTube watch time: 1 billion hours (it would take one person over 100,000 years to watch that much content)
- Total YouTube 2020 revenue: $19.7 billion (30.4% increase year-over-year)
- YouTube TV paying subscribers: 3 million
- YouTube Premium paying subscribers: 30 million
- Number of YouTube videos watched per day: 1 billion videos
- Hours of YouTube videos uploaded per minute: 500 hours

CHAPTER ONE:

CREATING YOUR YOUTUBE & ADSENSE ACCOUNTS

YouTube was founded nearly seventeen years ago by three PayPal employees: Chad Hurley, Steve Chen, and Jawed Karin. PayPal, if you remember, was Ebay's original payment processing system. How funny is it that the men who would start YouTube initially worked for PayPal, which was the payment service I used to run my Ebay business? It's a small tech world, indeed!

These three friends started YouTube in a small space above a Japanese restaurant and a pizzeria in San Mateo, California. It was Karin who was the star of the first video ever uploaded to YouTube: "Me at the Zoo."

Hurley, Chen, and Karin activated the domain name of "YouTube.com" on February 14, 2005, with the original concept of it being an online dating series. However, when that idea failed, the young entrepreneurs instead focused on making YouTube a place for non-computer experts to publish, upload, and stream videos through standard web browsers and household modems. In the beginning, video clips were limited to 100 megabytes with as little as 30 seconds of footage.

Everything changed a year later when Google purchased YouTube in 2006 for $1.65 billion in stock. After Google purchased YouTube, the site grew quickly, reaching 43% of the video market by the end of 2010. In the next few years, much was done to make YouTube more accessible to small content creators while also building the company up, including adding AdSense advertising payments for creators. Now people would upload for fun and make money from their videos.

Over the years, YouTube has grown from a small niche website to a platform with over two billion users worldwide. Today, creators, both large and small, produce videos for nearly two billion active users across the globe. And with nearly 122 million viewers logging onto the site every day, YouTube has shown no signs of slowing down, continuing to grow year after year.

Needless to say, YouTube has become a part of everyday life for a large population of people across the globe. With content that ranges from cooking, crafting, traveling, and family vlogging to gaming, beauty, style, news, comedy, finance, and business, there is truly something for everyone to watch on YouTube. And there is always a ready audience of YouTube viewers searching for videos.

So, you may be wondering, is there a place for YOU on this over-crowded site? The answer is YES! Anyone can start a YouTube channel today and work to make it successful. The key is that you must start your channel, and that is what you will learn how to do in this chapter.

YouTube makes it easy to upload videos, but it is Google that will pay you to do it. YouTube creators can make money on the site because Google owns the actual website itself. Google enabled channels to start making money from their videos in 2008. Some people, such as myself, look at YouTube as a way to bring in some additional income, while other people have made YouTube their full-time job.

Not only has this partnership between YouTube and Google been beneficial for channel creators, but it has also proved to be a lucrative opportunity for advertisers as they can reach customers across the globe for a fraction of the cost of television advertising. Think about it: Don't you see a lot of companies advertising on YouTube that you have never seen advertise on television? Google has given small companies a way to reach way more customers than if they were just running ads on TV.

YouTube currently runs ads on over a billion video views every week, giving a cut of the advertising revenue to creators. I will be talking in-depth about making money from your videos later on in this book. But before you can make any money, you must properly set up your YouTube and Google accounts.

Since Google owns YouTube and controls the AdSense advertising that pays you for your videos, **you must first sign up with Google to create a YouTube channel** that will earn you ad revenue. As I talked about in the *Introduction* to this book, when I started my first YouTube channel, I did not sign up through Google but instead registered through a different email account. Because I did not sign up for my first YouTube channel through a Google email address, that initial channel could not be monetized. Despite me consistently uploading videos and building an audience, I never earned a penny from those videos.

Fortunately, you do not have to worry about making the same mistake I made because today you can only get a YouTube channel through Google. If you already have a Gmail account through Google, you can skip this next section. But if you do not have a Gmail address, it is free and easy to set one up. Here is how:

GOOGLE ACCOUNT: To sign up for a Google account that will allow you to create a YouTube account and a YouTube channel, head to the Google Account sign-up page at **accounts.google.com/signup**. The registration process is quick, easy, and completely free.

The Google account page will allow you to create a **Google account** and then a **YouTube account**, a **Google "@gmail.com" email address**, and a **YouTube channel**, all in one place.

Simply follow the online prompts to complete the process. A Google account will first give you your own *YouTube account*, which will enable you to interact with other creator's content (such as subscribing to channels, giving videos a "thumbs up" or a "thumbs down," and leaving comments).

In addition to giving you your own YouTube account, it will also then give you your own *YouTube channel*. However, it is up to you if you want to activate your channel. Many people who have YouTube accounts never create their own channels; but the option is already built-in once you have an account. You will be prompted to create your channel by Google; the process is as simple as naming your channel. Do not worry if you are not ready to upload anything right away; the creation of your channel simply means that it is there if and when you are ready.

CHANNEL NAME: When you create your Google account, you will choose a user name. Most people make this their actual name, and I recommend that. You can then choose a different name for your actual YouTube channel.

Be sure to choose your YouTube channel name wisely. Google usually prompts you to make it the same as your account name, but you can select any name you like, just as long as another account is not currently using it. While you may just be starting on YouTube for fun now, you do not want to limit yourself from growing your brand in the future. There are many established, successful YouTube channels out there with names unrelated to their content because the people behind them never anticipated how large their channels would grow.

I named my first YouTube channel, the one that is no longer active, the same as my Ebay store name, the name that my reselling business was registered under. Since I was then only creating Ebay content at the time, that name made sense.

However, I ended up starting a now-defunct blog called "SeeAnnSave," where I posted about couponing and free samples. It was at this same time that I started my second YouTube channel using a Google account. I decided to delete my first channel, and I named my new YouTube channel "SeeAnnSave" to match my blog as I wanted to post money-saving videos in addition to my reselling content. Most of my followers on YouTube subscribed to my channel when it was "SeeAnnSave" and still call it that to this day.

Eventually, I closed my blog and changed my channel name to my name, "Ann Eckhart." Since I publish books under my own name, it made the most sense to "brand" all of my content under the same name, YouTube included. I also changed my social media handles to match.

"SeeAnnSave" became "Ann Eckhart" on YouTube, Facebook, Twitter, and Instagram.

While Google allowed me to make the name change, I had to completely rebrand everything, not only my channel name but channel artwork and logos. Plus, I had to change the names of all my social media accounts. It was a considerable undertaking, and while it was worth it in the long run, it took a lot of work. And as I mentioned, some people still see me as "SeeAnnSave." So, while you are not locked into the first name you choose, note that it is better to get it right the first time to save yourself the headache of changing everything later on. And if you cannot come up with anything unique, it is perfectly fine to use your real name.

Note that while you can change your YouTube channel name, you cannot change the URL yourself. The URL can only be changed by contacting Google directly. My main channel URL still ends with *seeannsave*, and my second channel URL ends with *seeannatwdw* as I initially started it as a Walt Disney World vacation vlog channel. While I changed my account names so that my primary channel NAME is now *Ann Eckhart,* and my second channel NAME is *Ann Eckhart Vlogs*, the URLs for both channels have not changed. It is confusing, I know!

To be honest, I still have not bothered to contact YouTube to ask about changing my URLs as, in the end, the website address itself does not matter too much. It is the name of the channel that I personally feel is important. Most viewers will either search for your channel name or just subscribe to your channel outright to find your videos; very few people will actually type in your channel's URL address, much less even know what it is. You can copy and paste your channel's URL to post it to your other social media accounts, which will allow people to simply click on the link to be taken right to your channel. No need to type in the actual address.

If you plan to make your YouTube channel your main website, you may want to purchase a dedicated URL from a site such as Go-Daddy.com and have it directed to your channel. For instance, I own the

URL AnnEckhart.com, which I have set to automatically direct users to my Amazon Author Page. My books are my primary source of income, and I want people to visit my author page above all of my other websites. However, if I was doing YouTube full-time, I could point the URL directly to my channel.

Owning the URLs to your channel name is a good idea in the long run. While you may be starting your channel just for fun, it may grow to the point where you want to "brand" your content. And if your Google AdSense grows to a significant amount, you will want to direct people to your channel; and that is much easier with a dedicated URL.

URLs are inexpensive to obtain and are something you will want to investigate as your channel grows. Choosing the ".com" version is the most logical, but if you find your channel becoming quite large, you will want to secure all the domains (.org, .net, etc.). And if your channel name is different from your own name, you may want to own the URLs for your name, too. I still own the "SeeAnnSave" URLs as well as the URLs for my own name.

SET UP YOUR ADSENSE ACCOUNT: While you used to start earning AdSense money right out of the gate on YouTube, in 2019, Google changed the requirements for becoming monetized (i.e., allowing you to place ads on your videos to earn a cut of the revenue from them). Now a channel needs to have 1,000 subscribers AND 4,000 hours of views before it can start making AdSense money.

While these new requirements are frustrating for new YouTube creators, you can get your channel to monetization standards rather quickly with dedication and consistency. I will go over ways to grow your channel later in this book. But first, more about AdSense.

According to Google, AdSense works in three steps:

1. You make your ad spaces available by pasting ad code on your blog or website, as well as placing ads on your YouTube videos.
2. The highest paying ads appear on your site as advertisers bid to show in your ad spaces in real-time auctions.

3. Creators are paid directly from Google, with Google handling the process of billing all advertisers for the ads that show up on your content.

As part of the AdSense Program, Google delivers ads to your blog/website/YouTube channel via their Google Ads system. Google then pays you for the advertisements displayed on your videos based on user clicks on ads OR ad impressions, depending on the ad type.

Creators cannot choose the ads that appear on their sites/videos. Google uses three methods to determine which ads are placed; according to them, these are:

1. **Contextual Targeting:** Google technology uses factors such as keyword analysis, word frequency, font size, and the overall link structure of the internet to determine what a site or video is about and precisely how to match Google ads to that particular content.
2. **Placement Targeting:** Under this format, advertisers can choose specific ad placements to run their ads. Ads that are placement-targeted may not be precisely related to a page's content, but are instead hand-selected by advertisers who have decided that there is a match between the products/services and what your readers/viewers are interested in.
3. **Personalized Targeting:** This offering enables advertisers to reach users based on their interests, demographics, types of websites they visit, the apps on their mobile devices, the cookies on their web browsers, the activity on their devices, previous interactions with other Google ads, and their own Google Account activity and information.

To monetize your videos, you will first need to become a **YouTube Partner**, which we will discuss in the next section of this chapter. As I mentioned, you now must have 1,000 subscribers and 4,000 hours of watch time before you can monetize your videos. However, if you have a blog or website, you will want to go ahead and sign up for a Google AdSense account now, as you can start earning money from ads on your site immediately. I was earning Google AdSense on my blog a couple of months before I started making money on my videos.

Simply visit **google.com/adsense/start** to begin the application process. Note that you will need to go through a verification process to qualify for an account, including providing your social security number for tax purposes and your bank routing information for direct deposit of your earnings. Some people are wary of providing this information, but it is the same as you would do if you were applying for a job. If you expect Google to pay you, then they will need your information for tax purposes.

Note that Google may also send you a PIN number via mail or email that you will need to provide to complete the application process. The process changes every so often, but Google will provide you with all the instructions to follow when submitting your application.

You can choose to have your AdSense earnings mailed to you or sent via direct deposit to your bank account. You must reach $100 in total AdSense earnings across all platforms (blog/website/YouTube) to receive a payout. For years, I had AdSense on both my blog and YouTube, so I easily met that $100 monthly threshold.

In late 2021, I shut my blog down and now only earn AdSense through YouTube. However, I still earn enough AdSense between my two channels to receive a monthly payout, which is automatically deposited into my bank account around the third week of the month.

Since AdSense is income, you do have to pay taxes on the money you earn. Fortunately, Google sends users tax forms every year. You can have your Google 1099 form mailed to you, or you can download it from your account. Do not worry about missing it: Google will notify you when the forms are available.

While AdSense is usually the most significant chunk of income for most channels, you also need to keep track of any sponsorship money you receive, as not all companies will send out tax forms for brand deals.

I have several affiliate marketing partnerships that never send out tax forms, but I still keep track of the money they pay me. I will talk more about managing your YouTube income later on in this book.

Once you have completed the application process and have been approved for an AdSense account, you can begin placing AdSense ads on your blog or website. However, you will have to wait to be eligible to join the YouTube Partner Program to start monetizing your YouTube videos. Joining the YouTube Partner Program is an additional step; do not worry, though, as Google will prompt you to do it once your channel is eligible.

BECOME A YOUTUBE PARTNER: After you have created your Google, YouTube channel, and AdSense accounts, there is one more step you will need to take before you can start earning money on your videos, and that is to become a **YouTube Partner**. Once your channel reaches 1,000 subscribers and 4,000 watch hours, YouTube will prompt you to sign up with their YouTube Partner Program.

According to YouTube, "The YouTube Partner Program (YPP) gives creators greater access to YouTube resources and features," including access to YouTube's creator support teams, copyright match tools, and monetization features.

The minimum eligibility requirements to join the YouTube Partner Program include:

- Following all the current YouTube monetization policies (these are frequently updated; once you are going through the application process, you will be prompted to agree to them)
- Live in a country or region where the YPP is available
- Have 4,000 valid public watch hours within 12 months
- Have more than 1,000 subscribers
- Have a linked AdSense account (again, this is an excellent reason to create your AdSense account even before you are eligible to apply to be a YouTube Partner as you will be ready to go once you meet the requirements)

Here is an abbreviate YouTube Partner Program application checklist:

1. Make sure your channel follows all policies and guidelines. When you apply, you will go through a standard review process to check if your channel meets these standards.
2. Enable 2-Step Verification for your Google account, which means you will protect your account with both your password and an additional device.
3. Have at least 1,000 subscribers and 4,000 valid watch hours on your channel.
4. Sign YTP terms to be notified when you are eligible to apply to become a YouTube Partner. You can do this manually, although YouTube will prompt you once you meet the subscriber and view thresholds.
5. Make sure you only have ONE AdSense account (you cannot have multiple accounts under your name).
6. Once you sign the YouTube Partner Program terms and connect your AdSense account, your channel will be put into a queue for review. Both automated systems and human reviewers will then review your channel's content before being accepted into the YouTube Partner Program. Note that it can take up to a month for your account to be reviewed; it depends on how many other accounts are in line before you and how much staff is currently available to conduct reviews.

MONETIZE YOUR VIDEOS: Your videos must be monetized for them to start earning income. Monetization means you are authorizing YouTube to place ads in your videos and that you agree that no copyrighted materials (music and video clips from TV shows, movies, or other licensed sources) appear in your footage.

If a piece of music accidentally makes it through, YouTube will likely still allow the video to play BUT will not allow ads to be placed on it, meaning you will not make any money from that particular video. These music copyright strikes happened to me frequently when I was vlogging my Walt Disney World vacations as much of the music played inside the parks was copyrighted. Fortunately, while I was not able to earn AdSense on those videos, YouTube allowed them to remain on their site. While I could have edited the music out, I chose to keep it in so that I could enjoy it when I watched the videos back myself.

Avoiding copyrighted music is a big reason why many vloggers do voice-overs on their footage. Many stores play music that, if picked up by your camera's microphone, will trigger YouTube to de-monetize your video. Do not worry if this happens; it will not negatively affect your other videos or prevent you from uploading again. It just means that the particular video, or parts of it, will not earn you any AdSense. If you do upload a video that triggers YouTube's copyright system, you can always delete it and re-edit the footage to take the music clips out. And once you have been filming for a while, you will learn where and when to avoid vlogging to prevent copyright issues.

Having an AdSense account does not automatically mean your videos will earn money. However, **you need to manually monetize each of your videos**. This is done in the **YouTube Studio** section of your YouTube account. You can access your YouTube Studio on your desktop computer or via their app. Note that the YouTube Studio app is separate from the YouTube app. While I have the YouTube Studio app downloaded on my phone, I prefer to use the YouTube Studio section on my computer as it is easier to access and edit all of the available features. The following directions are based on using YouTube Studio on a computer, not in the app.

Once a video is uploaded, simply click on it, choose the **edit icon** (it looks like a pencil), and then click on the "**$**" icon on the left-hand side of the page.

You will be brought to the **Video Monetization** page of the video you choose. Select **On** from the Monetization drop-down menu. A pop-up box will appear on your screen titled **Tell us what's in your**

video. Here you will need to confirm whether your video contains **Inappropriate language, Adult content, Violence, Shocking content, Harmful or dangerous acts, Drug-related content, Hateful Content, Firearms-related content**, and/or **Sensitive issues.** YouTube strictly controls videos that contain any of those types of content, so unless your videos contain any of them, you will simply check **None of the above** before hitting the **Submit** button.

You will then be taken back to the **Video monetization** page. Here you will want to check every box under the **Type of ads** section: **Display ads, Overlay ads, Sponsored cards, Skippable video ads,** and **Non-skippable video ads.** You will also want to check every box under **Location of video ads: Before video (pre-roll), During video (mid-roll),** and **After video (post-roll).** Click **Save** to finalize these options.

If your video is over eight minutes long, you will also want to click on the **MANAGE MID-ROLL** option found under **During video (mid-roll).** The advertisements that run in the middle of videos typically bring in the most revenue; so, you will want to make sure they are placed effectively in your videos. YouTube will automatically place them for you if you wish, but I personally like to make my own selections to ensure that the ads are not too close together. Sometimes YouTube will put in way too many ads or put all the ads right together, which will turn viewers off. Or sometimes they may not put enough ads in. Google also tends to insert ads into strange places within videos, such as at the very end of the video when viewers have already clicked off and are no longer watching.

I typically place my ads every six minutes to seven minutes, depending on how long the video is. For instance, I will place ads for a fifteen-minute video at the seven-minute mark. If a video is twenty-five minutes long, I might place ads at six, twelve, and eighteen minutes.

Placing ad breaks is easy; you simply **click on the "+" next to AD BREAK** and click to add as many individual placements as you want. Then, under the **PLACE AUTOMATICALLY** column, you enter in the time stamp for each. You can easily change these, so do not worry about making a mistake. You can also manually move each ad break at the bottom of the page. I will walk you through the step-by-step process I personally go through to monetize my videos later in this book.

Once you have your ad breaks where you want them, simply click on the **CONTINUE** button to confirm your selections. You will be brought back to the **Video monetization** page, but you are now done placing the ads on that video. You can now move on from that screen.

Make sure to go back into your old videos, the ones that were not monetized initially, to monetize them, too. The mid-roll ads are especially important, so even though it can be time-consuming to update your older videos with them, it will be worth it in terms of your earnings. Note that I will be going into more detail about how I upload, edit, and prepare my videos in "Chapter Nine: A Day in the Life" to give you an idea about managing your own uploads.

I know that the steps to set up and monetize your YouTube channel can seem overwhelming for new creators. Signing up for a Google account, an AdSense account, and a YouTube account, plus then applying for the YouTube Partner Program, all take time. And you need to make sure that the information you provide is accurate; after all, you are asking that Google pay you for ads that are placed in and on your content. It is almost like applying for a job, and you need to make sure your tax information is correct.

Be patient and make sure to follow all the instructions when you are filling out your applications. While signing up for a Google account and YouTube channel are automatic once you have submitted the forms, being accepted into the YouTube Partner Program can take a bit of time depending on how many other people are applying, too, as Google employees manually verify each account. Sometimes it only takes a week for accounts to be verified; other times, a few months. The wait can be frustrating, but once you are monetized and start earning money from your videos, I promise that it will be worth it.

And, remember that you only must do these tasks once. After you have all your accounts set up and have monetized your YouTube videos, you will be able to relax and enjoy the monthly deposits of money into your bank account!

YOUTUBE DEMOGRAPHICS

- 56% of users are male
- 44% of users are female
- 81% of U.S. adults use YouTube (in comparison, 69% use Facebook and 40% use Instagram)
- 82% of U.S. males use YouTube
- 80% of U.S. females use YouTube
- 95% of U.S. 18 to 29-year-olds use YouTube
- 91% of U.S. 30 to 49-year-olds use YouTube
- 49% of U.S. 65+ year-olds use YouTube
- 89% of YouTuber users come from outside the United States
- 51% of YouTuber users say they visit the site daily
- 37% of Millennials aged 18 to 34 are binge-watching YouTube daily
- YouTube is available in over 100 countries

CHAPTER TWO:

FILMING EQUIPMENT & SET-UP

My guess is that you are eager to read this section of the book because you want me to tell you exactly which camera you need to purchase to film your videos, the specific software you will need to edit your videos, and the perfect computer you need to edit your videos on, right?

Well, I hate to disappoint you as it just is not that easy, because while it would be nice if there were an all-in-one kit you could purchase directly from YouTube to start your channel, the fact is that there are hundreds of different setups available.

From different cameras and lighting equipment to editing software and computer systems, the options for filming, editing, and uploading YouTube videos are endless. And because new products are continually being released, there is always something new and better coming out.

However, while the options can seem overwhelming, I will be going over the basics in this chapter. I will give you ideas that range from using what you already own to investing in professional equipment.

You may find that you already own the tools you need to start your channel and that you do not have to purchase anything. I personally film, edit and upload videos on my iPhone, only switching to my laptop to finish some backend work before the video goes live. I have never owned an expensive camera or invested in editing software, and I have successfully built two channels without either.

When beginning any new venture, I believe that it is always best to start with what you already have before investing in anything new. This chapter will cover the types of products needed to film, edit, and upload

YouTube videos, along with examples of the current top products being used by creators. While I cannot tell you the exact setup to use, you will come away with the knowledge of what is out there and can then decide if you want to purchase any of it.

As I said, I do all my filming, editing, and uploading on my iPhone. In fact, I have only ever produced my YouTube videos using an iPhone. While I use apps to edit and upload my videos, I do use my laptop to complete the back-end production aspects for my channel. In the chapter "A Day in the Life," which appears later in this book, I will go over the step-by-step process for using an iPhone to film, edit and upload videos.

Setting aside the iPhone option, however, here is the necessary equipment you will need to run a YouTube channel:

CAMERA: Either an iPhone or a DSLR camera work best for filming YouTube videos. Many successful YouTube creators offer videos explaining their filming process along with the cameras they use. The best advice I can give you is to search YouTube for "best cameras to film YouTube videos" to see what comes up. Look for the most recent videos as those will give you information on the latest models. DSLR cameras range from $100 to well over $2,000.

As a basic guideline, you want a camera that can film in HD, whether 720p or 1080p. HD (high-definition) is the highest quality filming available for personal cameras and results in video footage that appears super crisp and clear. Most phones even film in HD these days, including the iPhone that I use. While I upload from my iPhone directly to YouTube, you will need to transfer your video footage to your computer via the camera's SD memory card if you use a stand-alone camera. Most creators who use this method rely on several memory cards to hold and transfer footage along with multiple batteries to keep their cameras working.

The most popular DSLR cameras currently being used to make YouTube videos are:

1. **Canon PowerShot G7 X Mark III:** A compact favorite of vloggers who film in 4K with a starting price of $600.
2. **Sony ZV-1:** Another compact video camera with 4K video resolution and a starting price of $700.
3. **DJI Pocket 2:** Offers excellent stabilization and straightforward operation with a starting price of $350.
4. **GoPro Hero2:** Popular because of its excellent stabilization, but you may want to add an external microphone. The price starts at $400.
5. **DJI Osmo Action:** Dubbed the "best YouTube action camera for novices," this waterproof camera is super affordable at under $200.
6. **Sony A6600:** One of the most expensive vlogging cameras available with a price of just under $1400. However, the battery life and storage make it popular for taking a lot of footage.
7. **Canon EOS M6 Mark II:** High-resolution camera with a starting price of $800.
8. **Panasonic Lumix GH5 II:** A great choice for both still shots and video but with a hefty starting price of $2000.
9. **Sigma fp:** The smallest full-frame camera also streams over USB and has a starting price of $1700.
10. **Samsung Galaxy S21 Ultra:** This phone also shoots in 8K, making it even better than the iPhone and with a starting price of $900.

If you already own a DSLR camera, see if you can use it for filming before deciding to invest in a new model. Again, do a YouTube search of the model camera you own and see if you can find tutorials about how to use it for filming videos. Chances are, there is at least one other person who is filming their videos with the same camera.

LIGHTING EQUIPMENT: If you intend to film vlog-style videos, i.e., footage of you as you go about your everyday life, then you will not have to worry about purchasing lighting equipment as you will be using whatever light happens to be available in the setting you are filming in, including natural light. Subsequently, if you have a large window that lets in a lot of natural light, you may be able to get away using just the window for lighting when filming sit-down videos inside.

However, even if you have a window with natural light, you still may want some additional lighting when filming. Many YouTube creators use studio lighting or a "ring light" when they film. Ring lights vary in size from tabletop to floor length. You can even purchase small ring lights that attach to your iPhone.

A search of "YouTube lights" on Amazon or other tech shopping sites will bring up a long list of options with prices from $30 and going up into the hundreds. Options range from single-light setups to complex multi-piece systems. A simple 10" ring light with a tripod stand is a great option to start with. As I suggested with cameras, search YouTube for "video lighting" to see suggestions from other creators.

Remember again that it is okay to start with what you have. A window and a lamp can do wonders for your video lighting. As you progress in your YouTube journey, you can always explore more expensive options if you feel they are necessary.

VIDEO EDITING SOFTWARE: These days, there are a lot of options when it comes to video editing software. I personally just use the free **iMovie** app on my iPhone to edit my YouTube videos. The iMovie app is also available for Apple laptops and computers. It is the most popular of all the video editing software as it is easy to use and comes with most Mac computer systems.

If you cannot or do not want to use iMovie, there are other options available, including:

- **Premiere Pro:** Available for both Windows and Mac, Premiere Pro is a favorite among YouTube creators. Subscriptions start at $21 a month and go up depending on features.
- **Final Cut Pro:** Available for Mac only for a one-time cost of $299.99 directly from Apple. Final Cut Pro is used by profes-

sional film editors and YouTuber creators but might be too so-phisticated for newbies.

- **Premiere Elements**: Available for both Windows and Mac for a one-time cost of $99.99 from Adobe. The simple interface is suitable for beginners as it is basically a watered-down version of Premiere Pro.
- **Pinnacle Studio 24**: Available for Windows. Prices start at $45 depending on the store. Pinnacle Studio is an excellent option for beginners.
- **CyberLink Power Director 365**: Available for both Windows and Mac starting at $29.99 a month. It is easy to use but also offers some advanced options.
- **Premiere Rush**: Available for Android and iOS from $9.99 to $52.99 per month. If you want to use your Android device for filming videos, this is the app you will want to use.

I suggest you do the same for video editing software as I recommended you do for vlogging cameras and lighting: Do your own research by seeing what other YouTube creators are using. A simple search of "best video editing software" on YouTube will yield you a lot of results. Many YouTube creators also put links to the items they use in the description boxes under their videos. See if some of the channels you currently enjoy watching have their editing software linked. You may find that you already have an editing program installed, one that came with your computer. Again, do a YouTube search of what you already have to see if other YouTube creators are also using the same program.

As with cameras, new software options and updates are continually being released. Plus, what software you need depends on the computer system you are using as well as your skill level. As always, see if you have something already installed on your phone or computer that will work before investing in new software.

COMPUTER: While I do the bulk of my YouTube work on my iPhone, I still utilize my laptop for my videos. I find it much easier to type in my titles and description box information using my computer versus my small phone keyboard. I also like accessing the **YouTube Studio** feature from my desktop to adjust my video specifics and monetization settings. While there is a YouTube Studio app on my iPhone, I still prefer the full version that is on the full website for completing specific tasks.

Fortunately, the YouTube Studio is accessible via the internet, and therefore works with both Macs and PCs. So, the computer you use for editing videos will work just fine for any other YouTube work you do as long as it has an internet connection. While I use my Apple iPhone to film, edit, and upload my videos, I use a Dell laptop with Microsoft software to access the internet and complete the backend work on my videos. Yes, I use a combination of both Apple and Microsoft products to manage my YouTube channel!

Note that while most large YouTube channels rely on Mac computers to edit, there are options for PC users as well. The Microsoft Surface, HP, and Dell computers (which I am a personal fan of) are used by many creators. A powerful and fast processor is the most critical factor you will want to consider in any computer you intend to use to run a YouTube channel (or, frankly, any online business).

If you are completely clueless about computers, simply visit a store that sells computers, such as Apple or Best Buy, and ask an associate which models have the most powerful and fastest processors, and let them know that you will be using the computer to edit and upload videos. A few years back, I needed to upgrade my laptop, and I asked an associate at Sam's Club which laptop had the best processor. He showed me their two best options, and I chose from there.

If you are already using your computer for gaming, it is likely powerful enough to handle YouTube, too.

INTERNET CONNECTION: Having a fast, reliable internet connection is essential if you intend to use your computer to edit and upload videos. I use my iPhone because the upload speed is considerably higher than if I uploaded videos on my laptop. If you are an avid

YouTube watcher, you have likely heard creators complain about the time it takes to upload their videos. So, if you are still using a dial-up modem to access the World Wide Web, it is time to upgrade.

These days, most internet service providers offer various speeds of high-speed internet. I recommend going with the fastest one you can afford. I firmly believe that time is money, and I need my internet connection to work as quickly as possible for me to run all my businesses, including YouTube.

TRIPOD: Tripods are another item that you might be able to delay buying or skip using altogether. If you plan only to vlog, then your hand will serve as your tripod. However, I do have a hand-help grip that I use on my phone when vlogging. It also works as a stand as it holds my phone upright when I am filming a sit-down video. There is no fancy tripod in my office: I just prop my phone up on a little stand on a table. And it cost less than $10.

I have seen YouTube creators prop their cameras and phones up in various ways: on stacks of books, nestled into cabinets, even on open shelves. If you buy a lighting kit, even a basic ring light, it will often come with a tripod that you can attach a camera or phone to. There are even portable tripods that come with a small ring light attached for use when you are on the go.

The benefits of a tripod are that they keep your filming device steady and set at the angle you choose. It can be a little more work to get the right angle when you are simply setting your camera onto a flat surface, or what you think is a flat surface. I run into issues keeping my camera steady on a table even when using my little stand. However, since I do not have a lighting kit, I also do not feel the need for a tripod. So, I manually fidget with my setup and go from there. See how you get by without using a tripod before buying one. There are all styles and sizes available on sites like Amazon that start at around $15.

WHAT YOUTUBE VIEWERS ARE WATCHING:

Views of videos with "beginner" in the title increased more than 50% between March and July 2020 as people stayed home due to the Coronavirus pandemic. What were people learning to do?

- Views of beauty tutorials increased nearly 50%
- Views of bike maintenance and repair videos increased by 90%
- Views of videos about raising chickens increased by 160%
- Videos about learning to play the guitar garnered 160 million viewers in a one-month time period
- Videos about container gardening garnered 6 million views in a one-month time period
- There was a 215% increase in daily uploads of videos relating to self-care
- There was a 458% increase in daily views for videos about making sourdough bread
- There was a 200% increase in daily views for videos about making bubble tea
- There was also a massive spike in views for videos about home haircuts

CHAPTER THREE:

FILMING TIPS

So, you have figured out which, if any, camera, lighting, editing software, computer, and tripod you will be using for your YouTube channel. That covers the equipment side of things. But there are other things to consider when you are filming YouTube videos that do not cost you any money but are just as important as those that do. And these are things that you will only learn through trial and error.

Quality: No matter what equipment you end up using to film, edit, and upload your YouTube videos, producing high quality videos is vital. As I have said several times, you do not need to invest in fancy equipment, at least not initially, so you must do the very best you can with what you have.

Even though I film on my iPhone, I still upload my videos in High Definition. iPhones let you film in 720p, 1080p, and 4K. Choose 4K if possible, although both 720p and 1080p are still excellent. The difference will come in the upload speed. I often do not have the time to allow my videos to upload in 1080p or 4K as I need my iPhone for other work. But if you have the option, always choose the highest resolution you can. YouTube and viewers both favor videos shot in the highest definition possible.

A Steady Hand: Nothing is worse than watching shaky camera footage, and I have been guilty of doing this myself while vlogging. A hand-held stand or tripod can help tremendously with this, which is why I now have a small handheld stand that is attached to my phone. If you are filming a sit-down video with the camera in one place, make sure it is on a flat, steady surface and that it is not moving around while you are filming.

Light: Lighting is the biggest issue for most YouTube creators, myself included. As I discussed earlier, natural light (either outside or through a window) can provide you with excellent lighting, although you may decide to upgrade to professional lights.

I rely on natural light when vlogging outdoors, and stores are often well-lit enough for me if I am vlogging while shopping. At home, I rely on a large window as well as a lamp. Whether you decide to invest in lighting or make do with what you have on hand, making sure your videos are well-lit is essential to your channel growth.

Speak Up: A big problem I see with many new YouTube creators is that their video volume is so low that I cannot even hear what they are saying. When filming, make sure you are speaking in a clear, loud voice. While you do not want to scream at your viewers, you do want to make sure they can hear what you are saying.

Ensure there is no background noise while you are filming, such as music or the television. Not only will background noise interfere with viewers hearing what you are saying, but often background noise is copyrighted, which means it may prevent you from monetizing your videos.

Turn your phone to silent and film in a quiet room with the door closed. If you live with other people, let them know when you are filming and ask them to keep noise and interruptions to a minimum. If you have a dog that barks or pets that will distract you, it may be best to place them elsewhere in your home while filming. I have dogs, so trust me when I say that they can be as distracting as young children when I am trying to film. Removing distractions also means your filming process will go much faster, which means you will be able to get back to your family and pets that much sooner.

If you are vlogging, make sure that your hand does not inadvertently cover up the microphone. Also, again, please be aware that most music is copyrighted, meaning you will not be able to monetize videos where background music is being played, such as in stores or tourist attractions.

For me, the most challenging part of vlogging is making sure no copyrighted music is picked up by the microphone. Nothing is worse than taking the time to vlog only to have YouTube put a copyright strike on the video due to music in the background. While the video will usually still be eligible to be viewed, it will be ineligible to earn you any AdSense.

Making sure that you speak clearly is also essential when you are filming videos. In my everyday life, I tend to talk fast and fill my speech with slang. But in order to appeal to a worldwide audience, I make sure that I speak slowly and clearly and avoid saying "like" and "um" throughout my videos. I also edit out sneezes and coughs. Having some water nearby is helpful to stay hydrated while filming so that your speech remains as clear as possible. Lip balm is also handy to keep your lips from drying out, which can negatively affect your speech.

Backgrounds: You have likely seen YouTube videos with professionally designed backgrounds, as well as those shot in what looks to be the home of a hoarder. While you do not need to spend thousands of dollars to make the background of your videos look like it came straight from a home decor magazine, you do want to make sure to film in a clean, clutter-free space with a simple backdrop.

For sit-down videos, I have a dedicated space in my office where I film. I have bookshelves behind me, and I change out the décor on the shelves seasonally. In the past, I will admit that my backgrounds were not as nice as I would have liked them to be, especially ones where there were piles of Ebay inventory behind me (although, in my defense, I was filming videos about Ebay!).

I am always trying to improve the quality of my videos, including my backgrounds. Note that if you are vlogging, you do not have to worry about creating a pretty backdrop as you will be filming yourself in whatever place you happen to be. However, you still want to be aware of your surroundings so that viewers are focused on you, not on what might be happening in the shot behind you. Try not to film other people in your vlogs, such as other customers inside of a store. While it is normal to catch a glimpse of a strangers back in a vlog, you do not want a video filmed with stranger's faces looking right into the camera.

One of my favorite backgrounds that I see many female YouTubers use is to film with their bed behind them and twinkle lights (the kind you put on Christmas trees) strung up around the bed frame or window. This lighting arrangement creates such a lovely scene for filming.

Other people film with the nicest part of their kitchen or living room behind them. Gamers and review channels often have bookshelves behind them full of neatly arranged products. You want your background to align with your content. For instance, if you film cooking videos, you will want to use your kitchen as your backdrop, not your dirty garage.

When in doubt, a plain wall always makes a great backdrop, especially if it is next to a window that provides natural light. If you are filming in a room with sparse decorations and furniture, test your audio to make sure there is no echo when speaking.

Suppose you are serious about making YouTube an actual business that earns you a decent income. In that case, you will want to consider dedicating a space for filming that is well lit and nicely decorated. However, if you are just starting out or you are only interested in making a bit of money from YouTube, do the best with what you have. Some of the biggest YouTube channels on the site today got their start with the creators filming while sitting on the floor of their bedrooms or even sitting in their cars with the cameras propped up on their steering wheels. As I have already talked about, start with what you have and build from there.

Camera Angle: Finding the angle from which you look your best on camera can be a challenge. Most of us feel we have a "good side," the side of our face from which we look a bit more attractive than the other. However, video is much different from still photography in that you move around on film and are not sitting in a stationary position. Therefore, it is more important to have the camera facing you directly and slightly above you. Having to look up a bit to the camera helps eliminate the double chin phenomenon!

As with background, the camera angle is something I have constantly been challenged by. While I do have an iPhone tripod, it is a flimsy thing that does not hold my iPhone very well. So, for sit-down videos, I just prop my iPhone up on some books or boxes. When vlogging, I now have a portable tripod that I can attach to my phone that also converts to a stand; I can just prop the stand up on a flat surface to film when I am on the go. And the handle helps me hold the camera steady when I am vlogging.

Of course, if you choose not to appear on screen, you need not focus on how you look but instead on how what you are filming looks like, whether it is a single stationary item or a moving scene. If you are filming cooking videos, for instance, you will want a tripod that holds the camera to look over what you are preparing. Or perhaps you can have someone else hold the camera and film you.

If you are doing close-up shots of your hands, make sure your nails are trim and clean. Nothing turns viewers off more than dirty fingernails. If you are filming your hands a lot, a professional manicure is a good investment, and it is also a tax write-off as it is a business expense!

Do not be surprised if your first videos do not look that great, as it takes time to learn how to film best. Try different angles and methods until you find what you are most comfortable with. I have put many of my older videos on "private," as the quality is terrible!

Keep It Classy: While you do not have to have your hair and makeup professionally done every time you film a YouTube video, you do want to take care of your appearance. Looking as clean and neat as possible goes a long way toward presenting yourself in the best possible light, even if you are simply wearing jeans and a plain tee-shirt.

If you smoke, do not smoke on camera. Avoid chewing gum while filming. Be aware of your language; swearing not only turns off viewers, but it can result in YouTube demonetizing your videos. And do your best to clean up your surrounding area. No one wants to see your overflowing trash can or a pile of dirty laundry in the background of your videos.

As I mentioned earlier, clean nails are so important, especially if you are filming close-up shots with your hands. Try to prepare yourself as you would if you were going on a job interview or first date when your clothing and appearance are at your best. Remember that you are trying to appeal to a broad audience of viewers and present yourself accordingly.

Preview Before Uploading: I have watched some horrible YouTube videos over the years, ones where the footage is dark, the volume is on mute, and the screen is jerky. I have even seen videos that were upside down! Before you make your videos live, preview them first. While they do not have to be up to the Hollywood standard of film quality, you want them to be as clear and steady as possible. If a video looks terrible to you when you are previewing it, imagine what viewers will think when you upload it.

Redo videos that are not of good quality. Practice makes perfect! I have re-filmed many videos during my time on YouTube. I know that having to re-film a video is frustrating, but I personally would rather take the time to completely redo a video than have a poor-quality clip be viewed by thousands and potentially millions of people. One poorly filmed video could cost me new subscribers. Therefore, I would rather have no video than a poorly filmed one.

YOUTUBE USAGE STATISTICS

- 15.5% of YouTube site traffic comes from the United States
- More than 70% of YouTube watch time comes from mobile devices
- YouTube users can navigate the site in 80 different languages
- YouTube is the world's second-most visited website
- YouTube is the world's second-most used social platform
- The average visitor to YouTube checks out 8.89 pages per day

- The number of channels with more than one million subscribers grew by more than 65% year-over-year
- The top genres watched by YouTube viewers are comedy (77%) and thriller/crime/mystery (60%)
- People watched 100 billion hours of gaming on YouTube in 2020
- India has the most YouTube users out of all the countries at 225 million
-

CHAPTER FOUR:

YOUR CHANNEL'S THEME & CONTENT

As I talked about in the "Introduction" of this book, my first YouTube channel was dedicated solely to my reselling business on Ebay. My videos focused on showing viewers the items I sourced at estate sales and thrift stores to sell online, along with all my tips and tricks for how to make money on Ebay. I did not really talk about anything else but reselling on that channel, and the people who subscribed to me were there to learn and/or talk about just Ebay, too.

I had also talked about how when I started my first YouTube channel that I signed up under a non-Google email (which, I remind you, you can no longer do; so no worries that you will make the same mistake that I did) and that I was not able to monetize my first channel. It took starting a second channel under a Google account that allowed me to earn AdSense income from my videos.

But to be honest, when I first started YouTube, I was not even aware that you could make money on the site. I was happy to just connect with other resellers and share what I knew. It was a small community, and it really helped me change the direction of my online selling business. If you will remember from the "Introduction," I was struggling to figure out a new direction for my business; and it was the videos I found on YouTube that helped me do just that.

However, I will also be honest and tell you that once I realized the possibilities of making money on YouTube, I made the leap and started a new channel. I ended up deleting the first channel and focused on my newly created one because, while I still enjoyed being on the site, I also wanted to earn money from my videos. However, just as I had with the first channel, my content still mainly centered around Ebay.

That changed over the years, as I have already discussed. From reselling content to couponing and traveling to cooking, my content across my current two active channels has been all over the place. And that has caused my channels to struggle. The constant change in not only content but in my posting schedule threw my YouTube algorithm for a loop, and YouTube punished me by suppressing my channels and placing low-dollar ads on my videos.

However, you do not have to make the same mistakes I have. I have learned the hard way what works and what does not; and this book is my way of passing that information on to you.

So, what is the biggest lesson I can share with you? Figure out your channel's theme and stick to it! Mixing business content with lifestyle content did not work for me, and my AdSense earnings dropped because of it. You need to figure out exactly what your channel is about in order to grow your audience and your income!

Now, that does not mean you cannot film different types of videos on one channel. It just means you need to stick to one TOPIC for your channel. For instance, I have many friends who are resellers who produce lots of different types of videos such as "shop with me" vlogs where they go sourcing, sit-down haul videos where they share what they purchased to resell, and even live sales where viewers buy directly from them in real-time.

But while the *styles* of videos may differ, the *topic* is always the same: reselling. Those who share lifestyle videos do so on a second channel. You have likely also seen this from some of the YouTube creators you follow. Many, like me, have a vlog channel and a channel for sit-down videos. Some focus on one topic on one channel, such as gaming or makeup tutorials, and something absolutely different on another channel, such as travel vlogs or parenting advice. You can cover different topics on YouTube as long as you cover each on different channels.

For me, I did best when I kept my reselling content to one channel and my lifestyle content to another. While some viewers watch all of my videos regardless of topic or channel, there are those who only tune in for the reselling videos and those who are only interested in non-reselling videos. Two different audiences plus two different topics equal TWO different YouTube channels.

So, the question is: What is the theme of YOUR YouTube channel? And do you intend to have one channel...or two?

Starting out, I would recommend you begin with just ONE YouTube channel. You want to master running a single channel before you ever even think about having two...or more. Yes, some people have three and even four channels. However, most YouTube creators only have one channel, so do not panic if you can only see yourself with one as it is totally normal!

If I were only making videos about Ebay, I would only have one channel. Reselling is such a small niche that it really does well with a dedicated channel, meaning it is best for me to put other content on a separate channel. But if the videos you intend to share all fall under the same general theme, such as lifestyle or gaming, then you will be just fine with all your content on one channel.

When I first started on YouTube, I viewed having a channel like having your own television network. I thought that my channel was like a network in my cable lineup. I believed that I could have different types of "shows" on my channel and that viewers would just pick the videos they wanted to watch.

Unfortunately, that is not the way viewers behave on YouTube. While you have NBC in your television channel line-up, it is likely that you only watch a few of the shows on the NBC network. However, you do not take NBC out of your television package just because you do not watch every show they air. You watch the shows you want to and simply ignore the rest.

YouTube, however, is different. Viewers look at the entire YouTube site as if it were a television network with the individual channels functioning as separate shows. They view YouTube like NBC; they have the YouTube app installed on their phone the way we have NBC in our television line-up. And just like NBC has different types of television shows, YouTube has different types of channels.

You have YouTube on your smartphone or computer, and you watch the "shows," i.e., the channels you like. However, you do not watch ALL the channels because you are not interested in all the different "shows." But you keep YouTube installed on your devices the same way you keep the various networks, such as NBC, installed on your television lineup.

Think of it like this: Say your favorite television show is *Friends*. *Friends* originally aired on the NBC television network, but it is now shown on many other channels and even streaming services via syndication. Imagine if you were happily watching an episode of *Friends,* but then the following show to air was *Law & Order*. Now, you may actually like *Law & Order*, but for this example, let's say that you do not. If you were watching *Friends* on your television or streaming service and *Law & Order* suddenly came on, you would just change the channel to a different show, right?

However, what if *Friends* had its very own dedicated television channel. You would need to subscribe to this channel separate from your other television channels. But since *Friends* is your absolute favorite show, you are thrilled to be able to subscribe to a channel that is dedicated only to *Friends*. But imagine one day that when you went to watch *Friends* on this dedicated channel, suddenly they also started showing episodes of *Law & Order*.

But now, this unique channel that you subscribed to just to watch *Friends* is showing you a completely different show, making it hard for you even to find the episodes of *Friends* that you want to watch. Would you stay subscribed to the channel or look for better content elsewhere? If this select *Friends* channel were a YouTube channel, most YouTube subscribers would unsubscribe once other shows were introduced. They would then find a different channel that focused only on *Friends*, leaving the first channel to die out.

Some YouTube viewers will subscribe and stay subscribed to channels because they like all or at least most of the "shows" (individual videos) that are being uploaded. However, if they start to dislike more "shows" (individual videos) than they actually like, they may unsubscribe from that channel and search out different channels to subscribe to, ones that provide them with the content they want.

You want to keep the audience you have and not drive them away, which is why it is so important to stick to the theme of your channel!

The most loyal of my YouTube viewers watch most videos I put out across both of my channels. Some viewers watch all the videos on both of my channels, while others only watch one channel. And still others only check in periodically depending on the video *topic*.

Trying to mix vacation vlogs in with reselling videos was a disaster for me as it confused my viewers as to what my channel (i.e., the "shows") was about, and I lost subscribers on both channels because of it.

These days I have my main channel, *Ann Eckhart*, where I film sit-down videos, and I have a second channel, *Ann Eckhart Vlogs*, for vlogging videos. Some viewers love vlogs; some viewers hate them. Some viewers love sit-down videos; other viewers hate them. Having two separate channels ensures that I keep both audiences happy and helps me attract new viewers who are looking for specific content (i.e., "shows").

However, at the end of the day, no matter what topic I am filming a video about or how much engagement I am getting between my channels, I try only to make videos that I WANT to make, ones that are FUN and INTERESTING to me. Even though I am now earning money on YouTube, the main reason I make videos is for my own personal enjoyment.

YouTube has improved my public speaking skills and increased my confidence. It has allowed me to network and make new friends with people I would have never met otherwise. And it has also helped me grow my book sales and make money from sponsorships. I make YouTube videos for FUN, and as a bonus, I also earn a PROFIT.

While I have covered a wide variety of topics in my years on YouTube, you are likely looking to only film videos on one subject. Do not follow the trends to go with what is popular. Make videos about what you LOVE and the subscribers, and AdSense revenue, will follow.

Some common YouTube channel themes and video topics are as follows. Note that the top ten lists were compiled at the time of publication and may change over the course of the year.

Beauty: Beauty bloggers and vloggers are all over YouTube, and they are some of the most successful channels on the site. Some YouTube "beauty gurus" have an accompanying blog to support their videos and to also earn more ad revenue from their websites, but that seems to be a less popular option than it once was. Instead, YouTube creators are now using Instagram and TikTok to promote their channels.

Regardless, if you love make-up and skincare, sharing your personal tips and tricks with others may be the perfect theme for your channel. And the opportunities for content are endless, as is the possibility of brands sending you free makeup products to test on camera.

In addition to doing make-up tutorials, beauty gurus also do first impression reviews of products, shopping hauls (from stores such as ULTA, Sephora, and Bath & Body Works), make-up storage, and make-up collections. Nail art also falls under the beauty umbrella, and there are entire channels devoted to nail polish storage and application.

The beauty category is very crowded on YouTube. Only start a beauty channel because you LOVE cosmetics as the chances of success are much lower versus other themes. However, if you are good at applying makeup and have a style that impresses others, the subscribers and ad revenue will follow.

Top 10 Beauty Channels:

1. James Charles
2. Nikkie Tutorials

3. Jeffree Star
4. Rclbeauty101
5. SaraBeautyCorner
6. Tati
7. Bethany Mota
8. Michelle Phan
9. Zoe Sugg
10. Grav3yardgirl

Business: A lot of my YouTube videos over the years have fallen under the "Business" category. In addition to reselling, I am also an author and have shared in videos about how I make money self-publishing. Other business topics I have made videos about include affiliate marketing, print-on-demand, and blogging.

If you are in a career that others are interested in, consider sharing about it on YouTube. You may even find yourself developing courses and paid Patreon groups based on your knowledge that you can also monetize. For instance, some of my fellow resellers have private groups where they share about where to source clothing from and which brands to buy. Viewers must pay for this special access, and it gives the channel creators an additional income stream.

Top 10 Business Channels:

1. The Google Business Channel
2. Marie Forleo
3. David Siteman Garland
4. Roberto Blake
5. TED Talks
6. Skillshare
7. Y Combinator
8. Chase Jarvis
9. Robin Sharma
10. Kevin Rose

Comedy & Pranks: Pranking has become a hot trend on YouTube, and there are some creators who are making big money putting on elaborate, often dangerous, and expensive stunts. And while this type of content is not easy to replicate, it can be done on a small scale through sketch comedy or single joke-telling. Videos such as these have been an avenue for comedians looking to break into the comedy business.

Top 10 Comedy/Prank Channels

1. Roman Atwood
2. Just for Laughs Gags
3. Magic of Rahat
4. Prank On
5. Remi Gaillard
6. Coby Persin
7. How to Prank It Up
8. Whatever
9. Improv Everywhere
10. Jack Vale Films

Cooking & Baking: Do you love to cook up new recipes or share your favorite baking creations with friends? If you enjoy being in the kitchen, you can share your culinary knowledge via YouTube videos. You do not have to be an expert chef, either; even the most straightforward recipes are popular on YouTube. In fact, sometimes simple is best as people are looking for quick and easy meal ideas.

I have posted several cooking and baking videos on my channels over the years; all my recipes are super easy to make, and I always get a lot of great feedback from viewers. Most of these videos are relatively short in length, but they are some of my top-earning AdSense videos!

Top 10 Cooking/Baking Channels:

1. Food Wishes from AllRecipes
2. Hiroyuki Terada

3. Chef Ricardo Cooking
4. Chef Buck
5. The Buddhist Chef
6. Chef Steps
7. Delish
8. The Stay at Home Chef
9. The Preppy Kitchen
10. Men with the Pot

Crafting: There is a vast crafting community on YouTube, so if you are a crafter, you will find others who share your passion. Whether you want to film tutorials or simply show off your craft supply hauls and projects, you will find an eager audience awaiting your content. Beading, scrapbooking, knitting, quilting, card making, and any other type of crafting and DIY category can make for great videos, whether they are tutorials or hauls.

The crafting community on YouTube is huge, so be sure to connect with other crafters who are making videos by liking and commenting on their videos, too. I am not a crafter myself, but I have done well with some DIY Dollar Tree tutorials.

Top 10 Crafting Channels:

1. Dazzle DIY
2. DIY Dalia
3. Lone Fox
4. Sheep & Stitch
5. Debi's Design Diary
6. Craft Life
7. Origami with Jo Nakashima
8. ThreadBanger
9. HGTV Handmade
10. Etsy

Fashion: Do you love to put together outfits? Do you like to style clothing you find at thrift stores? Do you enjoy reviewing new fashion brands? Then a fashion-themed channel may be an excellent fit for you! Figure out your niche and expand on that. Maybe you have an eye for vintage or like to create looks based on designer duds. Or maybe you enjoy styling the different body types of your friends and family. Whatever your personal style or mantra is, there is an audience for it on YouTube.

Fashion influencers also share tips on closet organization, their jewelry collections, and try-on hauls from trending online brands. Body positivity and plus size fashion are both popular trends online as people want to embrace their bodies and learn what works best on their frames.

Top 10 Fashion Channels:

1. Zoe Sugg
2. Tess Christine
3. Vanessa Ziletti
4. Jenn Im
5. Samantha Maria
6. Patricia Bright
7. Coolirpa
8. Mel Joy
9. Kalyn Nicholson
10. Amber Scholl

Gaming: Video game channels are among the most popular on YouTube, with the top creators earning millions of dollars a year just by live-streaming themselves playing games. If you love to play video games, you can turn your hobby into income on YouTube. Naturally, this will take a higher level of technology than simply filming on an iPhone. But if you are already into playing video games, you likely already know how to stream that content on your computer and share it on YouTube.

Top 10 Gaming Channels:

1. PewDiePie
2. VanossGaming
3. Markiplier
4. Ninja
5. Jacksepticeye
6. DanTDM
7. KSI
8. SSSniperWolf
9. W25
10. Syndicate

Gardening: If you have a green thumb, consider sharing your gardening skills on YouTube. Many people want to learn about plants, flowers, and vegetable gardening. Prepping and off-grid living are becoming very popular topics on YouTube, and gardening fits in with those genres. Share all your gardening information and watch your subscriber list (and AdSense money) grow along with your plants!

Top 10 Gardening Channels

1. Garden Answer
2. Growing Your Greens
3. Self Sufficient Me
4. Migardener
5. Urban Gardening
6. Garden Up
7. Gardening is My Passion
8. California Gardening
9. The Rusted Garden
10. Gardening Channel with James Prigioni

Hauls & Subscription Boxes: Love to shop? Share your shopping hauls with your YouTube subscribers. Even a trip to the grocery store to stock the fridge can make for an exciting video. Trader Joe's and Costco hauls are wildly popular. I film quite a few haul videos on my personal YouTube channel from stores such as Dollar Tree, Bath & Body Works, and Target, and they are always a big hit. Sometimes I even film "shop with me" videos and take my viewers along with me in vlog-style videos.

Subscription boxes fall under the "Hauls" category, and this is something I cover extensively on my main YouTube channel. Subscription box companies offer themed boxes filled with everything from beauty products to home décor. Subscribers can get these boxes monthly or quarterly, depending on the service. And opening these boxes has become extremely popular on YouTube.

Top 10 Stores for Haul Videos:

1. Target
2. Dollar Tree
3. Costco
4. Walmart
5. Sam's Club
6. Kohl's
7. JCPenney
8. TJMaxx
9. Burlington Coat Factory
10. Big Lots

Top 10 Subscription Boxes

1. Ipsy
2. Birchbox
3. FabFitFun
4. Boxycharm
5. Allure Beauty Box
6. Walmart Beauty Box
7. Glossybox
8. Stitch Fix

9. Loot Crate
10. Dollar Shave Club

Health: Another hot YouTube channel theme is health, specifically diet and fitness. Whether it is nutrition or weight loss, bodybuilding, or running, many people turn to YouTube to get in shape. Natural food and specialty diets (gluten-free, vegan, raw) are also popular video topics.

Top 10 Health Channels

1. Yoga with Adriene
2. FitnessBlender
3. Blogilates
4. POPSUGAR
5. ScottHermanFitness
6. Bradley Martyn
7. The Fitness Marshall
8. Kali Muscle
9. Pamela Reif
10. Matt Does Fitness

How-To: As I talked about in the filming equipment section, there are thousands of how-to videos on YouTube that cover nearly every topic you can think of, including how to film and edit YouTube videos. If there is an area or areas you are proficient in (computers, carpentry, crafting), creating how-to videos can be a great source of videos for your channel. Some channels are entirely dedicated to showing how to put together items purchased online.

I have recently relied on YouTube videos to show me how to build a shelf and to assemble a pressure washer, both of which I ordered on Amazon. Creators of these videos not only make money via AdSense but also from the affiliate links they provide. For instance, in the video I watched on the pressure washer, the creator linked the pressure washer in the video's description box. The creator then earned an Amazon commission from anyone who clicked on the link and made a purchase on the site.

A bonus of reviewing products is that you will be contacted by a lot of Amazon sellers who offer you a free product in exchange for you making a YouTube video about it. I have received free mattresses, pillows, vacuums, and small kitchen appliances from brands that simply want me to show their product in a video and give viewers the link to their website.

Top 10 How-To Channels:

1. Urban Gardening
2. Simone Giertz
3. The LockPickingLawyer
4. The Pedal Show
5. Dutch Pilot Girl
6. The 8-Bit Guy
7. Potato Jet
8. The Food Lab
9. Baumgartner Restoration
10. Primitive Technology

Lifehacks: If you like to scroll through social media, chances are you stumbled upon "lifehack" posts where people share shortcuts and tricks to do everything from peel vegetables to pack a suitcase. The possibilities of how to present this content are endless.

You can film one hack per video or put together lists such as "Top 10 Ways to Save Money Eating Out." A search of "lists" on YouTube will bring up countless options. From "Top 10 List of Disney World Rides" to the "List of Top 15 Movies of All Time," there is a list for everything. It may not seem like riveting content, but there is a considerable audience searching for it on YouTube.

Top 10 Lifehack Channels

1. 5-Minute Crafts
2. Wengie
3. The King of Random
4. Natalies Outlet
5. Troom Troom
6. Life Hacks & Experiments
7. HouseholdHacker
8. DaveHax
9. Mr. Hacker
10. Cute Life Hacks

Mommy Videos: Are you a mom-to-be, or do you already have little ones in the home? There are many other mothers out there who you can connect with, whether by merely sharing your baby's milestones or talking about what you feed your toddler. There are many women (and men!) looking to interact with other parents online.

Homeschooling videos are also popular, as are reviews of baby and children's products. Other videos that typically receive many views are kids clothing hauls, back-to-school hauls, and tips, and what presents parents are buying their kids for the holidays.

Top 10 Mommy Channels:

1. Cam&Fam
2. Britneyandbaby
3. Haylee And Family
4. She's In Her Apron
5. Sunkissed Mama
6. Life as a Mommy
7. StillGlamMom
8. Kee Does It All
9. Hard Working Mom
10. Lemonade Mom

Organization: Organizing is another hot YouTube channel theme. How to organize your house, office, car, kid's toys, crafts, garage, and basement can all make for great videos. If you excel at organizing, you may think there is no audience for this topic, but believe me that there are people out there who would love to watch you organize something as simple as a junk drawer! Organizing your home on a budget from dollar stores is something many people produce videos on, too.

Top 10 Organizing Channels:

1. Vasseurbeauty
2. Lavendaire
3. Love Meg
4. Rachel Talbott
5. Pick Up Limes
6. At Home with Nikki
7. Clutter Bug
8. Do It On a Dime
9. Rachelleea
10. Home Organization by Alejandra.tv

Restaurant & Food Reviews: If you are a foodie who loves to taste test the new dining and snack options in your area and when you travel, a channel dedicated to food reviews may be right up your alley. Whether you vlog while dining out, order fast food that you eat in your car, or do dedicated taste-testing videos at home, viewers gobble up food content!

Top 10 Food Review Channels:

1. Best Ever Food Review Show
2. TheReportoftheWeek
3. Mark Wiens
4. Trevor James
5. Tami Dunn
6. Family Food Dude

7. Gary20O
8. Strictly Dumpling
9. Mrhappy0121
10. BigDaddysWorld

Reviews: Do you love to read or go to the movies? Are friends always asking you to recommend your favorite video games or CDs? Do you always buy the latest gadgets? Millions of people turn to YouTube for reviews, so if you love books, movies, television, video games, music, and/or electronics, consider making a channel where you offer your opinions!

If you review products, you will soon start to be contacted by companies offering to send you free items in exchange for video reviews. In just the past few months alone, I have been sent a robotic vacuum, an air fryer, and a humidifier, all for free just for showing them on my YouTube channel.

If you do plan to do reviews, note that copyright issues will prevent you from using clips of movies, video games, television shows, or music. Still, you can hold up your own copy of a DVD or CD if you want some type of visual; or you can add still photos from the productions.

Another way to make money on reviews is to sign up for an Amazon Associates account and put your referral link in the description bar to the item you are reviewing. If someone buys something through your link, whether it was the item you reviewed or something else, you will earn a commission on their purchase. I will talk more about the Amazon Associates program later in this book.

Top 10 Review Channels:

1. Fun Toys Collector Disney Toys Review
2. Ryan Toysreview
3. Unbox Therapy
4. Blu Toys Club Surprise
5. Marques Brownlee

6. PSToyReviews
7. Vat19
8. Austin Evans
9. ToysReviewToys
10. Uravgconsumer

Tags: Tags are trendy amongst YouTubers. Tags are simply question and answer lists, such as "50 Random Facts About Me." There are tags galore on YouTube, and they give you an easy way to create content as all you must do is answer the questions. Tags are especially helpful if you are just starting out and unsure of what kinds of videos you want to make.

For a complete list of tags, check out my book, *The Big Book of YouTube Tags: Dozens of Fun Quizzes & Questionnaires for Video Creators,* which is available on Amazon.

Thrifting: Are you a bargain hunter who loves to score the racks at Goodwill for the best deals? Do you spend your Saturday mornings driving around town in search of garage sales? If you love to thrift, there is an audience waiting for you on YouTube! From shop-with-me vlogs to hauls and even DIY refurbishment of secondhand furniture, thrifting is a hot topic with an eager audience on YouTube.

Top Thrifting Channels:

1. Paul Cantu
2. Coolirpa – Upcycling Old Clothes DIY
3. itsHadrian
4. Threads Obsessed
5. Thrifted Living
6. ThriftersAnonymous
7. Katy P
8. Aaron Ramirez
9. There She Goes
10. Thrifting 101

Travel: Do you love to travel? Perhaps you take frequent road trips or cruises, or maybe you are an RV or camping enthusiast. There are lots of YouTube viewers who would love to see your travel footage, including your packing tips, dining recommendations, and money-saving advice. I have filmed many Walt Disney Vacation vlogs for my YouTube channel over the years, and they are always a big hit.

even mixed in with my other content.

Top 10 Travel Channels:

1. Fearless and Far
2. Drew Binsky
3. Hey Nadine
4. Kold
5. Lost LeBlanc
6. Mark Wiens
7. Phil Good Travel
8. Sorelle Amore
9. Brooke Saward
10. Fun For Louis

Vlogging: People worldwide chronicle their lives through vlogs, many doing so every day. Note that vlogging is very time-consuming and can feel like an invasion of privacy if you are not careful; however, many folks are earning a part-time and even a full-time income on YouTube by sharing 10-to-20-minute snippets of their daily lives. Note that you do not have to be a daily vlogger to have a vlog channel; you can film as many or as few vlogs as you would like, although it helps stick to a schedule, such as posting vlogs three times a week.

Suppose you enjoy vlogging but do not want to commit to a set vlogging schedule. In that case, you can simply vlog whenever you are doing something particularly exciting or during a "vlogging month" such as "Vlogmas" (vlogging for Christmas), "Vlogtober" (vlogging every day in October), "VEDA" (vlogging every day in April), or "Vlogust" (vlogging every day in August). I, myself, have done "Vlogust," "Vlogtober," and "Vlogmas" in the past.

The hard part about vlogging for me has been that the subscribers who love vlogs REALLY love vlogs and desperately want them to continue daily. It is a lot of pressure to keep up with daily uploads. For me, another downside to vlogging is that you are exposing yourself to more criticism and scrutiny than a regular sit-down or one-topic video might bring. Even when you only show 10-minutes out of a 24-hour day, viewers start to assume that they know everything about you and can either be overly friendly (i.e., a bit like a stalker!) or too critical.

Most daily vloggers start out interacting with viewers in the comments but stop doing so as their subscribers increase because they feel the need to guard their privacy more closely. If vlogging interests you, consider starting off by doing it once a week. You can always expand to more frequent vlogs if you decide you really enjoy doing them and do not feel like you are exposing too much of your personal life.

Top 10 Vlogging Channels:

1. Rachel Aust
2. Ali Abdaal
3. Nayna Florence
4. Holly Gabrielle
5. Azlia Williams
6. Roman Atwood Vlogs
7. Dan Is Not Interesting
8. Amazing Phil
9. Pointless Blog Vlogs
10. Tyler Oakley

CHAPTER FIVE:

HOW TO EARN MONEY ON YOUTUBE

So far, in this book, I have already discussed how you make money on YouTube via AdSense; but there are other ways you can bring in even more income with your videos. While AdSense will be your first money-making stream, it will likely not be your last as you grow your channel. In fact, the largest YouTube channels make most of their money from sources other than AdSense. For example, YouTuber Jeffree Star referred to his AdSense money as "extra" income on top of his beauty empire! And while you may not reach the level of fortune that Star has, you still have the potential to earn money on YouTube.

ADSENSE: At the beginning of this book, I covered the basics for monetizing your videos with AdSense, which you do as part of the YouTube Partner Program. But you must understand how AdSense works and how you can best utilize it on your channel in order to maximize your earnings.

AdSense is the route in which Google sells advertising. You have likely seen Google-branded pop-up ads on various websites. The money that advertisers pay for those ads is processed through AdSense. When you are monetized on YouTube, Google will run ads on your videos; just like ads that appear on text-based websites, the ads that appear on videos are purchased and sold through AdSense. You can think of Google Ads and AdSense as being one and the same.

Whether on a website or in a YouTube video, the Google ads that are shown to you have been matched to the content you are either reading or watching. For instance, if you are reading an article about travel, you will likely see ads for Disney World or cruise lines. The same is true for the YouTube videos you watch. These ads are created and paid for by advertising companies. These companies pay Google to run the ads, and Google then splits the money with the content creators, both on blogs and websites as well as on YouTube.

How much you will earn via Google AdSense depends on several different factors, such as the type of ads placed on your videos, how viewers respond to the ads, and the cost that each particular advertiser is paying Google to run their ads. The more a brand pays for an ad, the more you will make if people watch your video.

On YouTube, how much money a video makes is first determined by the **CPM**. CPM stands for **cost per 1,000 impressions**, and the CPM is what YouTube is able to charge advertisers for ads placed on your videos. While you are not paid the CPM amount, it is an essential factor in determining your **RPM**, which is your cut of the revenue. Again, CPM stands for what Google charges advertisers, and RPM is what Google pays you.

CPM's can be as low as 50-cents and as high as hundreds of dollars per one thousand views; it all depends on the video's content. Remember, the CPM is the amount of money that YouTube is charging advertisers, not the amount you are paid. Your RPM is usually half of your CPM, so a high CPM typically results in a high RPM.

As a YouTube creator, you are paid per 1,000 views on all your videos combined throughout the month. As an example, my general lifestyle videos earn around $12 CPM per 1,000 views. However, my reselling videos earn, on average, $35 CPM per 1,000 views.

Why the difference? Well, lifestyle videos are a dime a dozen on YouTube; there is so much competition in this category that content creators end up splitting the share of advertising between thousands of different channels. However, reselling is a tiny, niche category, but one with a loyal viewer base. And it is an audience that is specifically interested in money-making opportunities.

While finance companies will not find their audience on makeup tutorial videos, they will find them on videos about Ebay and Poshmark. Therefore, Google can charge those advertisers more as their audience is small. And since the reselling community on YouTube is relatively small, those of us who make reselling videos split the advertising dollars with fewer creators, making our CPM's higher. While there are hundreds of thousands of makeup tutorial videos, there may be less than 100 videos about how to list items for sale on Poshmark.

Bottom line: Niche content may not get as many views, but the advertising rates tend to be much higher, meaning your chances of earning money with a small audience are also much higher.

I have been fortunate that my CPM's have been on the higher side throughout my YouTube career. The average CPM across YouTube is only $4 per 1,000 views. However, this rate varies between every channel and can vary daily. My CPM's are constantly changing, going up and down depending on the money advertisers are investing in YouTube ads for the videos I make.

Once your YouTube videos are monetized to earn AdSense revenue, you can track your CPM in your account's **YouTube Studio** area. Simply click on the **Analytics** tab on the left side of the page to see your AdSense totals (you can customize the date range), and then click on **Revenue** to see your CPM. I personally like to check my numbers once a week to see how my month is going.

However, while your CPM number is important, it is your RPM, which stands for **Revenue Per Mile**, that is the amount of money you are actually earning. This metric represents how much money YouTube is paying you per 1,000 video views via Ads, Channel Memberships, YouTube Premium revenue, Super Chats, and Super Stickers (I will discuss each of these further along in this chapter).

CPM is the cost per 1000 ad impressions BEFORE YouTube takes its cut. RPM is your total revenue per 1000 views AFTER YouTube takes their cut. While your CPM is an advertiser-focused metric that only includes income from the ads on your videos that are monetized,

RPM is a creator-focused metric that provides for total revenue reported from all available sources. It also includes the total number of views from your videos. Your RPM number will always be lower than your CPM number as it is calculated after YouTube's revenue share and because it includes all views, even those on videos that, for whatever reason, were not monetized.

Confused? Do not worry, most people are! To be honest, I myself rarely dig too deeply into these numbers. I focus on tracking my revenue share in the **YouTube Studio section** of my YouTube account (simply click on your profile picture in the top right-hand side of your YouTube account and select "YouTube Studio" from the menu to find yours). By clicking on the **Analytics** icon on the left-hand side of the page, you will be able to bring up your **Channel Analytics**. From here, you can see your current revenue as well as several other statistics. You can also choose the date range, including:

- Last seven days
- Last 28 days
- Last 90 days
- Last 365 days
- Lifetime
- Current year
- Previous year
- Each of the past three months
- Custom

As I mentioned earlier, I personally narrow my display screen to the current month to see how my revenue is tracking for that particular month. Selecting any of the time options will narrow down your statistics on an overview page where you can see your **Views, Watch time (hours), New subscribers,** and **Estimated revenue.** I like to narrow down my numbers by clicking on the Revenue tab to see my RPM and

CPM. YouTube will also show you whether your numbers are up or down from the previous time frame via red arrows.

Note that the reporting of these numbers does lag a bit. You will need to wait until the end of the month when YouTube finalizes your revenue report to see what you actually earned. However, I still like to check my numbers to get an idea of where I am.

Further down the page under **Revenue** are even more helpful insights and statistics, including your estimated revenue for each of the past six months along with your top-performing videos via revenue for the current month. Noting your top-performing videos will show you what type of content your audience is reacting to, which will help you decide what videos to produce in the future.

You can also access your **Reach statistics** such as impressions, impressions click-through rate, views, and unique views. Under **Engagement**, you will find your watch time in hours and your average view duration. And finally, under **Audience**, you can see your unique viewers, average views per viewer, and the number of new subscribers.

All of these numbers, percentages, and statistics can be overwhelming. But the good thing is that you do not have to pay attention to them unless you enjoy digging through data. As I said, I only focus on my current running revenue balance and my CPM and RPM. And in truth, it is only my RPM revenue that is of any importance as that is how much money I will be paid.

Oh, and when does YouTube pay you? **Once you have earned at least $100 via Google AdSense, Google will initiate a payment to you the following month.** So, you will get paid your January AdSense revenue in February, typically during the third week of the month. You can choose to have your money directly deposited into your bank account. Or, for a fee, you can have Google mail you a check.

I choose direct deposit as it is automatic and so much easier than waiting on a paper check that I then have to take to the bank. Note that **if you earn $600 or more from AdSense in a year, YouTube will provide you with a 1099 form** to submit with your taxes. YouTube will notify you if you have a tax form available, which you can then print out. I will be going over YouTube accounting in the next chapter.

AFFILIATE LINKS: While AdSense is the primary way most people earn money on YouTube, there is another way to bring in cash from your videos, and that is through affiliate links. When you sign up to be an affiliate with a company, you can access affiliate links that will pay you a commission whenever someone buys an item through your personal link.

Amazon offers the most popular referral program, called **Amazon Associate,** which many YouTubers use, as well as bloggers and social media influencers. I have been an Amazon Associate even before starting my YouTube channel, as I would share my link via my other social media accounts. I then utilized the program on my blog. And today, I use the program in a Facebook group I have devoted to deals and freebies as well as on my business Facebook page and on Twitter.

By signing up as an Amazon Associate, you can create referral links to any of the products on Amazon's website. Then if you use or mention a product in your video and provide a link to it in your YouTube video description box, you will earn a commission if anyone goes through your link to purchase that product.

However, it is important to note that the person who clicks on your link does not have to purchase the exact product you link to; you will earn a commission on ANY items they buy once they are on Amazon's site if they got there using your referral link!

With Amazon being the largest e-commerce site globally, it makes sense that most YouTube creators are also Amazon Associates, as it is an easy way to earn additional money. Go to any large YouTube channel. You will likely find several Amazon Associate links in the description boxes below their videos, most often for the equipment they are using to film their videos. Those $1000 DSRL cameras can earn you a hefty Amazon Associate commission if you link yours under your videos!

The first link under my videos is to my Amazon storefront, which is a perk you are offered when you have 10,000 YouTube subscribers. This unique "influencer" Amazon Associate storefront gives me a dedicated page on Amazon where I can organize all of the products I offer. In addition to the books I write under my own name, I also create journals, planners, and notebooks that I sell on Amazon under the "Jean Lee" publishing name. Plus, I have a section for the reselling supplies I use and a section for the home products I often show in my vlogs.

I can easily direct viewers to this one link if they want to check out my books and other items. And I can quickly delete or add new items at any time.

In addition to the Amazon Associate program, there are all kinds of companies that offer affiliate opportunities. In addition to Amazon, you can sign up for FREE to be an affiliate with:

Adobe: Apply at adobe.com/affiliates.html. The Adobe Affiliate Program allows you to earn commissions when you promote Adobe Creative Cloud, Adobe Stock, and Adobe Document Cloud on your website, blog, or social media channels.

Audible: Apply at audible.com/ep/affiliate-intro. Earn advertising fees when you refer viewers to qualifying Audible products and memberships.

Brandcycle: Apply at brandcycle.com/. Brandcycle offers influencers the chance to partner with over 400 retail brands to access premium commission rates and exclusive offers.

Ebay Partner Network: Apply at partnernetwork.ebay.com/. Earn money by driving traffic and promoting sales across Ebay.

Honey: joinhoney.com/business/get-started. Earn money through this money-saving browser extension.

Movavi: Apply at movavi.com/partners/affiliate-program/. Earn money promoting the Movavi video software.

Rakuten (formerly LinkShare): Apply at rakutenadvertising.com/affiliate/. Work with the top brands across industries.

Rakuten also has a shopping portal, formerly called Ebates, that pays users a percentage back on their purchases. Shoppers simply create a free Rakuten account and then search the site for the retailer they want to shop from. They then click through to the store's website via Rakuten's link. Rakuten automatically tracks their spending, giving them a percentage back of their total purchase amount (anywhere from 1% up to 20%, depending on the site). Every three months, Rakuten automatically mails users out rebate checks. There are no points to track or special codes to enter; the entire process is automated on Rakuten's end.

While I utilize Rakuten for my own shopping rebates, I also use their affiliate program to make money. When you sign up for a Rakuten account, you are also given your own affiliate link to share on social media, including on YouTube. When someone signs up for Rakuten using your affiliate link and makes a purchase, you then earn $25. Any affiliate income you make is added to your own rebate total, and a check is then mailed out to you every three months. It is a safe, easy, and effective program to increase your overall YouTube earnings. And it is why you will see Rakuten affiliate links in many YouTube description boxes.

Shopify: Apply at shopify.com/affiliates. Earn commissions through your own Shopify store or by promoting others.

Sellfy: Apply at sellfy.com/affiliates/. Earn commissions by bringing customers to the Sellfy website.

ShareASale: Apply at shareasale.com/info/. Earn money by promoting partner offers and brands.

ShopHer Media: Apply at shophermedia.com/partners/. Earn commissions by directing shoppers to the various ShopHer brands.

ShopStyle Collective: Apply at shopstylecollective.com/. Earn money by sharing links to products you love. ShopStyle has thousands of brands available to promote.

Skillshare: Apply at skillshare.com/affiliates. Earn $7 for every new customer you refer to Skillshare, a website that hosts online classes and video lessons.

Skimlinks: Apply at skimlinks.com/. Skimlinks has a global network of 48,500 merchants that you can earn commissions from.

TripAdvisor: Apply at tripadvisor.com/affiliates. Partner with the world's largest travel site to earn 50% commissions for providing hotel booking links.

Twitch: Apply at affiliate.twitch.tv/. Twitch is an affiliate network specifically targeted toward streaming content.

REFERRAL LINKS: While affiliate programs pay you in cash, referral programs reward you in products or in credits toward paying for your purchases. For example, I belong to several monthly subscription box services, which I review on my YouTube vlog channel. If the company has a referral link, I will provide the link in the video's description box. Then, if someone signs up for the subscription using my link, I earn rewards. Sometimes it is points toward free products; other times, it is free boxes.

Since affiliate programs pay in cash, I generally prefer them over referral links. However, some companies offer both; and it is then up to me to decide which reward is better. In some cases, I use the affiliate link to earn cash; but in other cases, I may use the referral link to earn free products. It all depends on the reward.

For instance, I have a subscription to Grove Collaborative, which is a membership-based website that sells eco-friendly household products. They have both an affiliate program and a referral program. I choose to use my referral link to use the credits toward buying my own cleaning supplies. For me, the credits are more valuable than the affiliate money I could earn, even though the affiliate percentage is higher than the referral credit.

These days, nearly every brand and service seem to offer some type of referral program, including the major airlines and hotels, clothing and beauty companies, subscription boxes, and membership services. I belong to numerous referral programs, including FabFitFun, Causebox, and Thrive Marketplace, just to name a few.

Whenever you show an item of yours in a video, say a piece of clothing or a kitchen accessory, visit the brand's website to see if they offer an affiliate or referral program so that when you link the product in your video, you will have the potential to earn either cash or credit. If you have a blog or website, you can also put ads from these companies on your site to earn credits and free products that way.

Some popular referral programs are as follows. A simple Google search for each company name followed by "referral program" will take you directly to the pages to sign up. You may find that some will lead you to the affiliate programs listed in the previous section, but some will have their own dedicated program.

Acorns: This financial investment service specializes in micro-investing and robo-investing. Customers and those they refer receive a $5 bonus upon successful set up of an account.

Airbnb: Earn up to $30 in credits when you refer someone who completes a reservation as a guest or a host.

Alaska Airlines: Earn bonus miles when your referrals sign up and are approved for the Alaska Airlines Visa Signature Card.

American Express: If you have an American Express account, you can earn Membership Rewards for every successful referral.

American Giant: American Giant's tagline is "best hoodies in the world." Customers who successfully refer friends earn $20, while the referrals get a 15% discount.

Amerisleep: This natural memory foam mattress company will reward you with a prepaid Visa gift card when referrals order a mattress through your link.

Backcountry: This outdoor clothing seller offers both you and your referrals $10 toward future purchases.

Birchbox: Birchbox is the original beauty subscription box. Their referral program offers customers 100 Birchbox Points ($10) when someone signs up using their link. The referrals receive $9 off their first box with a minimum 3-month membership.

Blinds.com: This custom window treatment retailer gives both the referrer and the referral recipient $20 on all orders.

Blue Bottle Coffee: This coffee supplier gives customers and referrals $20 in credit toward future purchases for every order.

Boden: This clothing retailer has a large online presence. You can earn a $15 credit when someone makes a purchase through your link. The referral will receive 20% off their first purchase.

Brooklinen: This sheet and linen company offers a number of ways to earn credit, such as following them on social media and leaving reviews. Customers and referrals each receive 25% off their purchase of $100 or more.

BurnCycle: BurnCycle offers indoor cycling classes in Oregon and Washington. If you have one of these gyms near you, you can earn 15% when you successfully refer five people to complete a spin class. The people you refer get 15% off their next month's membership fee or class package.

Canva: This popular digital graphic design site gives customers credits toward premium images when their referral creates an account and completes a design.

Casper: Casper is an online mattress company that offers a rotating offering of referral credit offers such as Amazon gift cards. The referred customer receives 20% off their order.

Chase: Chase offers online banking and credit cards. Users can earn between 5,000 and 10,000 points (equal to $50 and $100, respectively) when they refer friends and family.

Choice Hotels: Earn points toward future hotel stays when referrals complete a stay with a participating hotel.

Coinbase: You can earn $10 worth of Bitcoin for everyone you refer.

Discover: Both customers and those they refer can earn statement credits via their referral program.

Dropbox: This online data storage service upgrades customers storage for every referral they make.

eBags: This online luggage store gives customers $10 in reward points for every referral. Referrals get 65% off their first order.

Everlane: This online clothing retailer gives customers $25 credit for every successful referral.

FabFitFun: As I mentioned earlier, I subscribe to the FabFitFun subscription box, which means I am given referral codes to share. I earn $15 in referral credits for everyone who signs up using my link. The referrals receive $10 off their first box.

Fabletics: This Kate Hudson founded company offers a fitness wear subscription. Subscribers are given a referral link that gives new customers 50% off their first order. For every friend you refer, you earn $10 in-store credit.

Farm Fresh To You: This organic fruit and vegetable delivery service give customers a unique Refer-A-Friend link to share that gives referrals $15 toward their first order. In return, you receive a $25 credit.

Getaround: Called the Airbnb of car sharing, referral users earn $20 credit for anyone who signs up using their link.

Girlfriend Collective: This activewear brand sells clothes from recycled materials and offers a pair of free leggings when someone uses your referral link to make a purchase. The referrals are given $10 off their purchase of $95 or more.

Glossier: This online cosmetics company awards you with $10 in-store credit when a referred customer clicks on your link, creates an account, and places an order. The referrals receive 10% off their first purchase.

Groupon: Groupon is a deal site that offers discounts on products and services, both online and local. Users can earn $10 in Groupon Bucks for every referral that purchases a Groupon.

Hanna Anderson: This children's apparel company gives customers 20% off a future order when referring friends and family. Referrals receive 20% off their first order.

HelloFresh: This meal subscription service rewards customers with a $20 credit for every successful referral. The referral gets $40 off their first box.

HotelTonight: Earn money toward your next booking when you share your referral link.

Hunter: Hunter makes pricey boots and outerwear. You can earn $15 per referral when they make a purchase. The referral gets $15 off their first order.

Intuit QuickBooks: Earn a $100 pre-paid Visa card for every person who subscribes through your link.

Lime Lush Boutique: This online women's clothing shop offers you $20 in-store credit for every successful referral. The referral gets 20% off their first order.

Lyft: Another popular ridesharing program, Lyft rewards when someone uses their referral link. You can choose cash, Lyft credit, or a combination of the two.

Madison Reed: This hair care company has a "share the love" program where you can earn a $15 credit for every referral that signs up using your link. The referrals receive a $15 discount on their first purchase.

Marriott Hotel: Earn up to 50,000 bonus points when you refer up to five new customers per year.

MeUndies: This online underwear shop rewards you with $20 in credit for each successful referral. Referrals get 20% off their first purchase.

Minted: This online stationery company offers users $25 in credit when someone they refer makes a purchase of $100 or more. The referral also receives $25 off their first order.

Moo: This online print and design company offers two ways to earn rewards through referrals. When you refer a friend, they have the potential to win a $20 gift card. If you refer a business with a minimum of 10 employees, the reward increases to $150. The referrals themselves get 24% off their first order.

Naturebox: An online healthy snack shop that rewards customers with $10 off future orders for every friend they refer. Your referral link offers people 50% off their first order.

Outdoor Voices: Earn $20 to spend at this activewear retailer for every referral who signs up. The people you refer get 20% off their first order.

Peapod: This online grocery store allows you to share your referral link on social media or via email. Your link offers people $50 off their first two orders. In return, you will receive $25 toward your next order.

Rebecca Minkoff: This luxury women's retailer has a Refer-A-Friend program that gives both you and the referral $20 for each successful referral.

Robinhood: This online investment app rewards you and your referrals free stock of up to $500 a calendar year.

Quip: Quip is a subscription-based dental company that provides customers with electric toothbrushes, refill packs, toothpaste, and dental floss. Earn $5 in credits for every referral you make. The referrals also earn $5 credit for every successful purchase they make. Quip also rewards you with $5 in credit when you invite your dentist to join.

Seated: This restaurant reservation app gives customers and those they refer credits to apply toward future reservations. When you have five successful referrals, you will be upgraded to "Seated Partner," where you can earn bonus rewards.

Shoes for Crews: This online store sells slip-resistant footwear to the workforce. Referrals reward both individuals with a $10 credit.

Shyp: This online shipping and fulfillment company serves e-commerce stores and small businesses with brick-and-mortar locations. Users can earn credit toward future shipments when they share their referral code.

Soylent: Soylent is a meal-replacement product. Their refer-a-friend program rewards you in points when referrals spend $24 or more on their first subscription order. Points can be redeemed on your own purchases. Referrals receive $10 off their first subscription of $24 or more.

Swagbucks: One of the first points-based rewards companies offers customers gift cards and cash for completing activities online. Their referral program awards you 10% of whatever your referrals earn.

Thinx: This online retailer has a strong focus on women's health. Customers receive $10 for every customer they refer, and referrals are given $10 off their first order.

Timberland: Timberland sells rugged shoes and boots. You can earn 20% off your future purchase when someone you refer makes a purchase. The referrals also receive 20% off their first order.

Uber: The popular ride-share company rewards you with discounts and free rides when people sign up using your link.

Uniqlo: This Japan-based clothing retailer gives customers $10 for every successful referral. The referrals receive $10 off their first order.

Vera Bradley: Vera Bradley specializes in bags in fun prints. Their Refer-A-Friend program rewards both you and the referral with 20% off a future purchase.

Verizon: If you are a Verizon customer, you can utilize their Refer-A-Friend program to earn up to $100 on a prepaid Mastercard when you successfully refer a new customer.

Vistaprint: This online print company sells a wide variety of custom stationery products. Customers receive $10 when they successfully refer a new customer.

Vonage: Vonage is a "voice over internet protocol" service provider. Customers earn a $50 gift card for every referral who signs up for their service.

Winc: An online wine subscription service gives you two complimentary bottles of wine when anyone uses your link to place an order. The referral will also receive $22 of wine with their first purchase.

SPONSORSHIPS: In addition to earning money through Ad-Sense, Amazon Associates, Rakuten, affiliate links, and referral links, you can also bring in cash through sponsorships. A sponsorship is when a company pays you to film a video. If a company has a product to promote, they will send you the item and pay you to film a video about it. If it is a service, the company will pay you to talk about their company.

A major cosmetic brand recently sponsored me. They sent me a box of their makeup to review, and I filmed a video of me testing it out. On top of giving me free products, they also paid me a sponsorship fee. Note that you need to disclose sponsored videos, both verbally within the video and in the video's description box.

The more subscribers a channel has, the more lucrative sponsorships can be. Many large YouTube channels make more money from sponsorships than they do from AdSense. It takes a while to build up a large enough audience to start attracting sponsors; I began receiving sponsorship offers when my channel hit 5,000 subscribers (although I started getting offers of free products when my second channel barely had 1,000 subscribers). But it depends on what kind of content you are producing and how many actual views your videos typically get. Most brands will judge your channel based on the average number of views your videos receive, not necessarily by your subscriber numbers.

While most sponsorships come from companies contacting creators directly, you can also sign up with sponsorship companies to connect you with potential sponsors. These companies include, but are not limited to:

AspireIQ: Formerly called Revfluence, AspireIQ markets itself as the leading influencer marketing platform. They connect brands with influencers, paying creators to create content that drives traffic to the companies they represent, including Bed Bath & Beyond, Marriott, Walmart, and Nike. In addition to YouTube, you can also earn money from them on your blog/website, Facebook page, Twitter feed, and even Pinterest. Learn more at aspireiq.com.

Channel Pages by FanBridge: Channel Pages has no minimum YouTube subscriber count to qualify for signing up. They have an extensive collection of brands, both big and small. Their platform lets you connect with brands and apply for collaboration opportunities with other channels. Learn more at channelpages.com.

Content BLVD: Content BLVD works with cosmetics brands such as Urban Decay and Skin & Co. Content BLVD works exclusively with YouTuber's who are paid to review the brands they represent. Not only can you get free products, but you will also be paid to make a video about them. Learn more at contentblvd.com.

Grapevine: Grapevine works with influencers who have 10,000 YouTube subscribers or 10,000 Instagram followers. However, even if you haven't reached that level of followers, you can still sign up with them. They help you choose brand deals based on your channel size, niche, and demographics. Some of the companies they work with are Walgreens, NYX, and Remington. Learn more at grapevinevillage.com.

Izea: There are no minimum subscriber counts in order to sign up with Izea, a company that works to connect food, fashion, beauty, and lifestyle brands with content creators. Some of the companies they represent include Subway, Levi's, and Ebay. They also offer freelancing gigs. Learn more at izea.com.

TapInfluence: TapInfluence has no minimum subscriber requirement and can connect you with food, fashion, beauty, and lifestyle brands such as WhiteWave Food, MtoM Consulting, and Stella & Chewy's. Their "open bidding" feature lets you bid on projects that match your content. Learn more at tapinfluence.com.

YouTube Brand Connect: Formerly called Famebit, the newly re-branded YouTube Brand Connect offers YouTube creators sponsorships for big brands, including Canon, Sony, and Adidas. YouTube Brand Connect is currently invite-only for channels with 25,000 subscribers. If you become eligible, YouTube will notify you within your YouTube Studio interface.

Note that the companies listed above are not the only places to obtain sponsorships, as some brands work independently to connect with creators. Once you start gaining subscribers, you will likely start to be contacted directly by companies who either want to send you free products to review or who are willing to pay you a sponsorship fee for mention in a video.

A critical part of sponsorships is settling on the amount of money you expect to be paid. If you are just starting out, you cannot expect a company to pay you thousands of dollars to sponsor a video. In fact, in the early days of your YouTube career, you may only be able to film videos in exchange for free products.

However, as your channel grows, you can start to expect payment for your services. Most brands will try to pay you as little as possible, if anything at all; so, you must go into YouTube with the mindset that your time is valuable. If a company approaches you with a sponsorship offer, it is because they feel you are a good fit for their brand. Therefore, they should already expect that they will need to pay you to film a sponsored video for them.

While sponsors look at your total subscriber count, they also look at how many views your videos average. How much you will be comfortable charging is a question only you can answer, although a good formula to start with is $0.05 to $0.15 per view or $50 to $150 per 1,000 views. Some brands will ask you for your rate, while others will propose a fixed price. In the end, only you can decide the rate you will charge.

You must have policies in place before accepting a sponsorship deal. You want to agree on:

1. When will the video go live?
2. How long will the video need to be in terms of length?
3. Does the brand need to approve the video before it launches?
4. When and how will you receive your payment?
5. Will the company be providing you with a script?
6. Will the company be providing you with links and discount codes to share with your viewers?
7. Will you be given free products to show in your video?
8. What else does the company expect from you? For example, will you be expected to share the video on social media?
9. Will the company be requiring that you use specific hashtags?
10. Will the company be providing you with disclosure text to place in the description box of the video?

Some companies will ask very little of you other than filming a video discussing their product or service, while others will expect you to sign a contract and complete numerous steps in order to get paid. I have had some brands just mail me a product to show in a video, while others have demanded I sign a contract with very detailed instructions on how, what, where, and when to film. The more a company expects of you, the more you should expect from them in terms of compensation.

SELLING YOUR OWN PRODUCTS: From tee shirts and coffee mugs to courses and books, YouTube creators frequently sell their own merchandise, also called "merch." My YouTube channel drives traffic to my books (in addition to this book, I have written several books about selling on Ebay and making money online) and to my Ebay store, and I also have print-on-demand items that I sell, both on Amazon and TeePublic. I provide links to all my products in the description boxes below every video I post in hopes that some of my viewers will purchase my products. I do not think I would be as successful as I have been with my books if it was not for YouTube driving traffic to them and subscribers actually buying them.

Creating your own merchandise is easy on sites like TeePublic and TeeSpring. I create my designs using Canva software, which requires a small monthly fee. For text-only designs, an app like WordSwag is free and easy to use. Or sites like Vecteezy and Creative Fabric offer subscriptions to access graphics you can use for commercial use.

I have a TeePublic store that is linked under my YouTube videos, and I sell items ranging from tee-shirts to coffee mugs there every week. I also have merchandise that I have created in TeeSpring that appears below my videos. The TeeSpring offerings are in direct collaboration with YouTube, hence why the links are under the videos.

If you have a nickname or tagline, considering slapping it on a tee-shirt or coffee mug and offering it up for sale to your YouTube viewers to help grow your brand and bring in extra money.

CHANNEL MEMBERSHIPS: Channel memberships are a relatively new feature for YouTube creators. Memberships allow viewers to join your channel through monthly payments, enabling them to receive benefits such as special emojis, badges, stickers, and videos only offered to members.

Note that there is a minimum eligibility requirement that creators must meet before being able even to apply to offer Channel Memberships. As of this writing, requirements include:

- Your channel must have more than 1,000 subscribers
- Your channel must be enrolled in the YouTube Partner Program
- You must be over 18 years of age
- You must be located in one of the eligible countries (Argentina, Australia, Austria, Bahrain, Belarus, Belgium, Bolivia, Bosnia and Herzegovina, Brazil, Bulgaria, Canada, Chile, Colombia, Costa Rica, Croatia, Cyprus, Czech Republic, Denmark, Dominican Republic, Ecuador, El Salvador, Estonia, Finland, France, Germany, Greece, Guatemala, Honduras, Hong Kong, Hungary, Iceland, India, Indonesia, Ireland, Israel, Italy, Japan, Kuwait, Latvia, Lebanon, Liechtenstein, Lithuania, Luxembourg, Macedonia, Malaysia, Malta, Mexico, Netherlands, New Zealand, Nicaragua, Norway, Oman, Panama, Paraguay, Peru, Philippines, Poland, Portugal, Qatar, Romania, Russia, Saudi Arabia, Senegal, Serbia, Singapore, Slovakia, Slovenia, South Africa, South Korea, Spain, Sweden, Switzerland, Taiwan, Thailand, Turkey, Uganda, United Arab Emirates, United Kingdom, United States, Uruguay, Vietnam)
- Your channel has a Community Tab
- Your channel is not set as "made for kids"
- Your channel does not have a significant number of ineligible videos (such as set as being "made for kids" or with music claims)
- You are complying with YouTube's terms and policies

If you are eligible and choose to offer Channel Memberships to your viewers, you can select from several "perks" to features, including:

- Badges
- Emojis

- Private videos
- Live chats
- Downloads of content
- In-person meetings
- Contests
- Sweepstakes

Some creators also offer physical items that they mail out to their channel members, such as stickers, cards, shirts, and more. You can offer memberships priced as low as $0.99 per month all the way up to $99.99 a month. Creators receive 70% of membership revenue after applicable taxes and fees are taken out.

YOUTUBE PREMIUM: YouTube Premium is a subscription service that costs $11.99 per month and allows viewers to:

- Watch videos ad-free
- Download videos to watch offline
- Play videos in the background while using other apps
- Access the YouTube Music App
- Listen to music ad-free
- Download music to listen to offline
- Play music in the background while using other apps
- Watch ad-free YouTube Kids videos as well as the ability to play offline
- Listen to Google Play Music (for most countries)

Creators do not have to subscribe to YouTube Premium for their videos to be included in the subscription. And while ads will not be appearing on your videos if someone with a YouTube Premium account is viewing them, you will still receive a cut of the membership fees that are being paid to YouTube by subscribed viewers.

SUPER CHATS & SUPER STICKERS: Super Chats and Super Stickers allow viewers to connect with creators during live chats. Viewers can purchase Super Chats to send creators money; their comment then appears highlighted in the chat. Viewers can also purchase Super Stickers, which are a digital or animated image that pops up in the live chat feed. Channels with many subscribers can often earn quite a bit of money from viewers sending them these chats and stickers during live stream videos. For those with huge channels, a Super Chat is often the only way for a viewer to be noticed by a creator during a live stream as the creator will hear a notification sound when they receive a donation as well as the comment or sticker being highlighted in the chat stream.

PATREON: Patreon is a membership service that some YouTube creators utilize to earn additional income. Some channels use Patreon essentially like a tip jar, while others have multiple membership levels, each with varying degrees of perks such as exclusive videos and merchandise.

TIP JAR: Just as some creators use Patreon as a virtual tip jar, you can also collect tips on your blog, website, or YouTube channel via several ways, including by providing your audience with your PayPal, Stripe, or Venmo email. A simple message such as "If you would like to support my channel with a virtual tip, you can send it to" with the email address associated with your account.

YOUTUBE FINANCIAL STATISTICS

- YouTube generated $19.7 billion in revenue in 2021, a 30.4% increase year-overyear
- YouTube generated $6 billion in revenue in Q1 2021, a 49% increase in year-over-year
- The number of channels earning five figures per year on YouTube grew more than 50% year-over-year
- YouTube creators with 500-5,000 subscribers charge on average of $315 per sponsored video
- YouTube creators with 500,000+ subscribers charge on average $3857 per sponsored video

- YouTube pays $18 per 1,000 ad views on average; however, most YouTube channels only earn $.50 per 1,000 views
- Over the past five years, YouTube had paid out over $2 billion to content creators

CHAPTER SIX:

YOUTUBE ACCOUNTING MADE EASY

I know what you might be thinking as you start this chapter: "I want to start a YouTube channel, not worry about accounting!"

Well, that is the catch when it comes to making money online: Like it or not, you must pay taxes on the money you earn, and that includes what you earn on YouTube! While it would be great to keep all the AdSense money you earn every month, if you earn more than $600 in a year from your channel, you will be giving a cut to Uncle Sam every year.

The good news is that YouTube bookkeeping is relatively easy! Unlike my Ebay business, where I have considerable expenses and forms to keep track of, it is much easier to manage my YouTube income and expenses. However, it is still important that I do as there are tax write-offs associated with running my YouTube channel.

Before I dive deeper into how I manage my YouTube accounting, please note that I am not an accountant. I PAY an accountant to file my taxes for me. But I do keep track of my income and expenses throughout the year. Be sure to consult with an accountant or tax professional in your area regarding your own tax obligations. The following advice is just that: advice.

But even with an accountant handling my tax filing, I still need to provide him with my actual numbers. As I mentioned, I do track my income and expenses throughout the year, so that come tax time, I have my numbers all ready to hand over to my accountant. My entire bookkeeping system can be found in my **2022 YouTube Creator Planner:**

All-In-One Channel Organizer Plus Mileage & Financial Ledgers, which is available exclusively on Amazon.

The accounting ledgers provided in the planner are broken down into two sections: Income and Expenses. Income is the money you earn from YouTube, and expenses are the money you spend on your channel. There are monthly ledgers and year-end ones to make the entire process easy.

Every month, I record the following streams of income from my YouTube channel:

- **AdSense:** Money paid directly to YouTube creators from Google from the ads placed on videos. If you earn more than $600 in AdSense in a calendar year, Google will issue you a 1099 form.
- **Sponsorships:** Any money that a company pays you to promote their products/services on your channel. Most companies do not provide 1099 forms, so you will manually need to track this money.
- **Patreon:** Nowadays, it is common for YouTube creators to have paid Patreon membership groups where they provide exclusive content.
- **Donations:** Some YouTube creators accept donations from viewers, so be sure to log in any money gifted to you by viewers.

Note that I do not earn money from all these sources every month; I just include them in the planner so the fields are there for those who may. I consistently earn AdSense and sometimes also earn money from sponsorships. I no longer have Patreon or donation options.

Every year, YouTube sends me a 1099 form for my AdSense. If you earn more than $600 in a year, Google will issue you a 1099 form. You can choose to have them mail the 1099 form to you, or you can print it off online. Do not worry: YouTube will notify you if and when your 1099 form is ready. But even if you do not meet the $600 threshold, you may still need to claim what you did earn on your taxes. Be sure to consult with an accountant or tax professional in your area, as some states have different rules than others.

As for sponsorships, it depends on the company if they send you a 1099 form. Many do not, but you still need to track that income. I have personally never received a 1099 form from a sponsor, but I have also never made a large amount of money from sponsorships. You will need to ask any company that sponsors you what their policy is.

Patreon sends users 1099 forms if they earn $20,000 in a year. However, if you live in Illinois, they will issue you a 1099 form if you earn $1000 or more in a year. If you live in Maryland, Massachusetts, Vermont, or Virginia, the threshold to receive a 1099 form is $600 or more in a year. But like sponsorships, even if you do not receive a tax form, you will likely still need to claim any money you earn from Patreon. Again, check with a professional in your area, as the laws vary by state.

Some YouTube creators set up donation links, and while it may not amount to very much, you still need to account for it.

After you have tallied your gross income total, you next need to make a note of your expenses. Since Google pays YouTube creators advertising royalties, YouTube is looked at as a business by the government. While this means you need to claim the money you make, it also means you can claim expenses as tax write-offs.

In my planner, I have space for you to record the following expenses:

Bank Fees: It is wise to set up a separate bank account for any business you have, including YouTube. Most banks do charge fees for checking accounts, but credit unions typically do not. If you already have a bank account, it is okay to stick with that for now. But if you start earning a large amount of money on YouTube, you will definitely want to consider a dedicated account just for your channel earnings.

Phone/Internet: Your smartphone and internet connection are essential items for running your channel, which means you can claim these as expenses. From the phone itself to the plan you are on, along with the internet connection you pay for, all are deductions you can claim on your taxes.

Equipment: Even the most basic YouTube setup (um, that would be mine, ha-ha!) requires equipment. Cameras, tripods, lighting, computers, and printers are all business expenses you can claim as business deductions.

Software/Subscriptions: Paying for editing software and graphic subscriptions can add up. Fortunately, these are business deductions for YouTubers. Do not forget any apps you pay for, as you can claim those, too.

Office Supplies: Copy paper, pens, toner ink for your printer - these are all items you are likely using to manage your YouTube channel, so keep track of what you are spending on them.

Postage: If you do giveaways on your channel, then you are likely paying money to ship out prizes. Keep track of how much you spend on postage as well as any shipping materials (boxes, envelopes, packing materials). Note that printing a shipping label online at usps.com costs less than taking packages into the Post Office.

Advertising: I occasionally run Facebook ads for my YouTube channel. Since I have a Facebook page, it is easy to set up advertisements on the site. I also include business cards and any other promotional materials I buy in the "advertising" category.

Props: If you are spending money on your video backgrounds or buying things to show on camera, these items count as props, and you can claim them come tax time.

Giveaways: Giveaways can be a great way to grow your channel (I will talk about this more in the next chapter), so keep track of any money you spend on prizes.

Travel: If you travel at all for your channel, you can claim those expenses. I once claimed a Disney World vacation because I was researching a book!

Meals: You can claim any money you spend on meals if you are doing so for your channel. For instance, maybe you are treating a fellow creator with whom you are collaborating out to lunch. Or perhaps you are reviewing a restaurant for your channel. Keep those receipts and write down how much you spend.

Taxes: As your channel grows, you may find that you are making enough money that you will need to pay quarterly income tax. Quarterly income tax is something many small businesses schedule to avoid paying one large lump sum at the end of the year. I pay both state and federal quarterly taxes four times a year. An accountant can set this up for you. My accountant prepares the forms I need to mail in; all I have to do is write the checks and address the envelopes. This does not mean that I will not still owe taxes, but it helps with a big chunk of it. If I earn more than anticipated, I will then still owe come tax time. But if my income was down, I may end up with a refund. Taxes are unavoidable, so again, consult with an accountant!

Mileage: You may not think you are driving much for your YouTube channel, but you likely are. If you are a vlogger, you definitely are. But even if you only film sit-down videos at home, you are likely still driving a bit in relation to your channel. Whether it is going to the Post Office or buying giveaway prizes at a local store, be sure to track your mileage as you can deduct it come tax time. There are several free apps you can download to your smartphone to track your mileage. My favorite is MileIQ which tracks your miles just by the movement of your phone while in the car.

At the end of every month, add up your gross income numbers and then add up your expenses. Subtract your expenses from your total gross income to get your NET PROFIT for the month. Then at the end of the year, tally up each individual category to get your year-end numbers. These total numbers of income and expenses are what your accountant will need to prepare your taxes.

Having to hand over a chuck of your hard-earned money to the government is not fun for anyone, but it is a fact of life. And if you want to be successful on YouTube and make money on the site, taxes are something you will have to deal with. Find a good local accountant who understands small home-based businesses that have 1099 forms to file. The expense of a good accountant is worth it to have your taxes filed correctly!

HIGHEST PAID YOUTUBE CREATORS:

1. Ryan Kaji: 9-year-old children's content creator earned approximately $29.5 million
2. MrBeast: Expensive prank channel earned approximately $24 million
3. Dude Perfect: Sport-trick content creators earned approximately $23 million
4. Rhett and Link: "Good Mythical Morning" series creators earned approximately $20 million
5. Markiplier: Gaming channel creator earned approximately $19.5 million
6. Preston Arsement: Gaming channel creator earned approximately $19 million
7. Nastya: Russian children's content creator earned approximately $18.5 million
8. Blippi (Stevin John): Children's content creator earned approximately $17 million
9. David Dobrik: American comedy and stunt creator earned approximately $15.5 million
10. Jeffree Star: American beauty creator earned approximately $15 million

CHAPTER SEVEN:

MARKETING & PROMOTION

If you really want to establish a presence on YouTube and earn money from your videos, you will have to do everything you can to promote your channel and build your brand. YouTube is a social media platform, and you want to use all the other social media sites available to you to draw traffic to your videos. More traffic equals more views, which in turn equals more AdSense revenue, and that can also lead to sponsorship opportunities as your channel grows.

Fortunately, the social media sites that will bring you the most traffic are all free and easy to use. And it is likely that you already have accounts on some or even all of them. And once you get into the habit of promoting your videos via social media, it becomes second nature and is a quick step to complete every time you upload a new video.

Setting up your various social networking sites is yet another reason why it is so essential that you choose the best YouTube channel name possible right out of the gate. You want to be known under the same name everywhere to establish your brand.

I am now "Ann Eckhart" on my main YouTube channel as well as on Facebook, Twitter, Instagram, TikTok, and Pinterest. I use the same photo across all my sites, too, so that no matter what website someone is browsing, when they see "Ann Eckhart" and my picture, they know it is me. My second channel may be called "Ann Eckhart Vlogs," but I still promote it under my "Ann Eckhart" brand as it is just easier to have one social media account identity across each of the various sites.

However, both of my channels and their accompanying social media sites used to have different names: SeeAnnSave and SeeAnnAtWDW, respectively. Renaming everything was a huge hassle. And while it made sense for me to do since my content changed drastically, hopefully you will be sticking with one "brand" for your YouTube journey.

While I do YouTube for fun, it is also a business for me. Everything I create in regards to my channel is done to promote it as a brand. My videos drive traffic to my books, and my books drive traffic to my channel. My social media sites promote both my books and my YouTube channel. It is a trifecta of promotion: YouTube, books, and social media all working together to drive traffic to each other, which grows my audience and results in more book sales, more affiliate income, and more AdSense dollars.

This chapter will cover all of the possible ways you can market your videos to grow your channel. Note that you do not have to do any of these if you do not want to, and you certainly do not have to do all of them. However, some social media promotion is beneficial in promoting your videos. So even if you are not currently using social media, give it a chance in order to grow your channel.

BLOG/WEBSITE: Most successful YouTube creators have coordinating blogs or websites, some even starting those sites before creating YouTube channels. What is great about a blog or a website is they are additional ways to earn AdSense dollars. When you have both a blog and a monetized YouTube channel, you have two AdSense income sources. Plus, you can place other ads on your site, some through affiliate and referral programs and others directly from selling advertising to companies.

Before I started my last blog, I had dabbled in blogging a few different times on Blogger, which is Google's blog platform. I originally had a blog dedicated solely to my Ebay business. However, when I started *AnnEckhart.com*, I closed the former blog and moved all content to the new website.

Note that I am speaking in the past tense as in 2021, I chose to close my blog down. Since I was only using it as a place to post my new YouTube videos, I honestly did not see it serving a purpose anymore. It had become expensive, and I was constantly having site issues; so, shutting it down worked best for me.

However, I still want to talk to you about having a blog as it can be beneficial for your channel. If YouTube were my primary income, I would likely have kept my blog. But even though I no longer have it, I will explain to you how the site worked for me when I had it so that you can see how it could work for you, too.

The difference between my first Ebay blog and my recent *AnnEckhart.com* blog was that my Ebay blog was just a blog, whereas my AnnEckhart.com blog was technically a website that hosted my blog. In essence, it was a blog ON a website.

Confused? Do not worry; I was, and still am sometimes, when trying to explain the difference! Even today, I struggle with whether to call *AnnEckhart.com* a blog or a website. In the beginning, I called it a website, but toward the end, I called it a blog, even though it was technically a website, mainly because the term "blog" is more prevalent in the social media world. Oy!

To put it simply, a blog that is on a free platform such as Blogger or WordPress is just a blog. However, a website is an actual site that you own that utilizes blogging software. *AnnEckhart.com* was my website, and on my website, I used WordPress blogging software.

When you have a blog on a free site, it is not yours but instead belongs to the company behind the site you are using, which means that it could be shut down at any time, resulting in you losing all your content. And while Blogger and WordPress have been around for years and show no signs of going anywhere, the risk is still there that you could eventually lose all your content.

I had my blog set up through Bluehost (bluehost.com), and I used WordPress software. This is a different setup than just starting a free blog on a site such as Blogger or WordPress. Since I was using a hosting company, I actually OWNED my website. I paid Bluehost for all their hosting services and features, one of which was the WordPress blogging software. I decided to go the route of paying for my site so that it could not be taken down. If Blogger or WordPress were to suddenly shut down (not likely to happen, of course, but you never know), I would still have had my website as I own it through a hosting company.

Having an actual website that incorporates a blogging platform also allowed me many more options for customization. I could do a lot more with my Bluehost site than I could if I were going directly through WordPress, for example. Bluehost offers numerous free plug-ins for the sites they host, including those for placing AdSense ads. I simply installed one of the free AdSense plug-ins, clicked where I wanted ads to show, and the ads were automatically placed. I then earned AdSense money from those ads. And I could change the ad placements and sizes at any time.

I looked at my website as my "homepage" for everything I did. I could share my videos there as well as my books. I could post updates, which automatically went out to anyone who subscribed to receive them. I had my affiliate and referral links organized along with links to all of my social media pages. I even had an entire section devoted to my recipes, which were very popular with my followers. When I spoke with someone who asked about my YouTube channel or books, it was much easier for me to direct them to *AnnEckhart.com* than it was trying to explain how they could find my YouTube channel or my books on Amazon. *AnnEckhart.com* was the leading portal for my "brand.

Today, however, the AnnEckhart.com URL points to my Amazon Author Page. Since my books are currently my primary income, that is where I want people to go. If I was doing YouTube full time, I could easily point the URL to my channel. When you purchase URLs through sites such as GoDaddy.com, you have the ability to point your URLs to any site you like. And it is easy to change, too. On the day I decided not to renew my blog, I went into my GoDaddy account and pointed my URLs away from the blog and over to my books.

So, do I miss having a blog, especially for sharing my YouTube videos? While having a coordinating blog or website can be helpful, note that it is not a requirement. Many successful YouTube creators do not have any sort of website. While they may utilize some additional social media sites to promote themselves, many focus solely on their channel. In fact, there are quite a number of successful YouTube creators who ONLY utilize YouTube and barely, if at all, post on any other social media platforms.

When you are just starting out on YouTube, focusing solely on your channel certainly makes the most sense. After you have been on YouTube for a while, if you feel like you really want to grow your channel, you can start branching out to other social media platforms. You will want to explore all of the free social media sites first before deciding if you want to invest money into your own website.

When I had my Ebay blog on Blogger, I did not put anything significant on it; I just posted about new listings in my store and had the links to my social networking sites. I rarely even promoted the blog; I just maintained it so that if anyone happened to stumble across it, they would hopefully click through to my Ebay store.

However, my *AnnEckhart.com* blog was a business for me as I earned income through affiliate advertising and referral links, not to mention that it drove traffic to my YouTube channel and to my books. If my site had been on a free blogging platform, all of my information could have been lost at a moment's notice. However, as long as I kept paying my website maintenance fees, my content was safe and belonged to me.

Oh, the cost? Yup, having a website costs money! I spent several hundred dollars every year maintaining my hosting contract as well as plugins and URLs. I no longer feel the cost is worth it for me, but again, it may end up being different for you.

If you do decide to pursue having your own website, I personally would not even bother creating a blog on a free platform as you do not want to spend time driving traffic to a site that you might eventually want to change. If you are absolutely sure that you want to start your own site, I would go straight to a paid version so that you own it right out of the gate. A website is something that can wait until you are further along in your YouTube career.

If you decide to go with a paid website, do your research as there are many companies out there to choose from. I went with a large company (bluehost.com) because I wanted my blog to be the centerpiece of my brand and because I wanted to utilize several forms of affiliate advertising on it. However, there are a lot of low-cost website options out there. For instance, you can not only register for website URLs on GoDaddy (godaddy.com), but they also offer website hosting along with easy-to-create websites and blogs. I personally use a GoDaddy website that is attached to a fiction pen name I use. It is a basic site but comes with my URL cost and does the basic job I need it to do.

So, which should you choose? A free blog or a website? Or no site at all? That is a decision only you can make. Having a blog or website for your YouTube channel is NOT a requirement. In fact, it may be more work than is worth it for you. And as I talk about in the next section, you may find that a Facebook page can just as easily act as your "website."

However, if you do decide to set up a blog or website, it does not have to be complicated. Think of it as the "home" page for your brand to provide the links to your videos and all your social networking sites.

One significant benefit of having a blog is that you can run giveaways there. YouTube no longer allows you to host giveaways on your channel or videos. You are not allowed to tie in giveaway requirements to your videos, meaning you cannot instruct people to enter a giveaway by subscribing to your channel, giving a video a "thumbs up," or leaving a comment. You can announce giveaways in your videos, but you must direct people somewhere else to enter.

Hence, a website comes in handy for hosting giveaways as people can enter directly on your site. When I did giveaways, I first wrote up a post detailing the prize and entrance requirements and directing people to enter by leaving comments on the post. I then randomly drew the winner or winners from the entries. Or I sometimes used a site such as Random.org to insert code that allowed people to enter the giveaway quickly and made it easy for me to draw the winner. Because people had to submit their email addresses to enter the giveaways, I just emailed the winner to obtain their mailing address to send them their prize.

It is important to note that Facebook has the same policy as YouTube regarding giveaways in that you cannot run them on their site on a public page. You can, however, run them if you have a private Facebook group, which I will discuss in the next section. Just note that if you plan to do giveaways, you will need to have a site other than YouTube or Facebook to host them. You can, however, run the giveaways on Twitter or Instagram. I personally favor Instagram as it is so easy to contact the winners via Instagram's messaging system.

Note that in addition to posting updates on your blog, you will also need to maintain it. If you allow visitors to leave comments on your posts, you will want to make sure to respond to them. You also want to maintain all links to ensure they are active and up-to-date so that people do not click through and get an error.

You will also want to secure a URL or several URLs for your website. I use GoDaddy.com to purchase my URLs; I own not only *AnnEckhart.com* but also several iterations of my name as well as my Ebay store and other businesses I own. While .com is the most popular suffix, there are many other options you might want to consider owning as well, such as .org, .info, .net, etc. Each of these additional options comes with an added price.

It is an added expense to purchase URL addresses, but if you are serious about building a brand, it is an investment you will want to make. You can purchase URLs for a minimum of one year, although you will likely save some money if you commit to a longer-term.

Here are the top sites to purchase URLs, also called "domain names," from:

Bluehost: I have talked about how I used Bluehost to host my blog, but you can also register URLs through them. They are the official

WordPress hosting partner; WordPress was the software I used to run my blog. Learn more at bluehost.com.

Domain.com: In addition to purchasing URLs, Domain.com also offers a Website Builder and email account. Learn more at Domain.com.

GoDaddy: Probably the most recognizable name in the domain business, GoDaddy manages over 77 million URLs for over 18 million customers. As I have mentioned, it is the site I use for purchasing my domains, and I also utilize their website and email services. Learn more at godaddy.com.

HostGator: HostGator offers domains along with website hosting and is an ideal site for beginners. Learn more at hostgator.com.

Network Solutions: In addition to domain registration, Network Solutions offers web hosting, a website builder, security tools, email addresses, marketing, SEO services, and IT support. Learn more at NetworkSolutions.com.

FACEBOOK: If you want to "brand" yourself and your YouTube channel, you will want to set up a Facebook page. Facebook offers more ways to connect with your audience than Twitter, Pinterest, and Instagram combined. And if you do not want the hassle of maintaining a blog or separate site, a Facebook page can efficiently act as your dedicated "website."

YouTube makes it easy to share your videos to Facebook as there is a Facebook "share" button located under all videos. Simply click on the Facebook icon, link your YouTube and Facebook accounts together, and you can then share your YouTube videos on your personal and/or business page.

Note that while you may have a personal Facebook account, you will want to set up a Facebook PAGE for your YouTube channel. A Facebook business page is different from a personal Facebook page, although you first need to have a personal Facebook account and page to set up a business page.

A business page is one people "like," while a personal page is one where people "friend" you. A personal Facebook page limits the number of "friends" you can have, but you can have limitless "likes" on your business page. Plus, having a business page also allows you to separate your personal and public life.

My personal Facebook page is private and is only for my personal friends and family to see. However, my "Ann Eckhart" Facebook page is public; anyone can view it and "like" it in order to be notified when I post there. Since my public page is a business page, it also allows me to accept sponsorships from companies that pay me to post about their products on my feed.

As your YouTube channel grows, you will likely find that viewers want to "friend" you on your personal Facebook page. Even if you are not promoting your personal page, it will still be easy for most people to find. Unless it is a subscriber you have gotten to know very well, I strongly encourage you NOT to add subscribers as friends on Facebook. You want to maintain privacy with a division between your personal and public/business life.

While many of my friends and family do "like" my Facebook business page, not all do. Keeping my personal page private protects me and my friends and family from having their information exposed to my business pages followers. You can try to "hide" your personal Facebook page by not using your photo in your profile picture and by using a different name, such as your first and middle name or a maiden name if you have one.

I use my Facebook business page to promote my YouTube videos and books, and I save my personal information for my personal Facebook account. While it is hard to turn down friend requests from well-meaning people, I only accept Facebook "friend" requests from my actual friends and family for safety and security reasons. YouTube subscribers and readers of my books need to "like" my Facebook business page to connect with me.

I have set up my personal Facebook page with the tightest security settings to protect myself. I have also turned off the private messaging settings on my business page so that people cannot send me messages.

When I allowed people to message me, I found myself inundated with long notes from people wanting advice on Ebay, help with publishing, or just someone to chat with. While most of these messages were harmless, it took a lot of my time and energy to deal with all the questions.

Again, just as it is hard to deny friend requests, it can be hard to ignore messages from well-meaning followers. However, I always remind myself that I am not just running my businesses, including my YouTube channel, for profit. In other words, I need the money to pay my bills! And while YouTube has never been my primary source of income, I am continuously growing my brand for the long term. Therefore, I treat everything I do as a business. I also need to protect myself and my family by guarding my personal information as much as possible. Hence why I am so protective over my online privacy.

A Facebook page needs "likes" to grow. While it can take a while to build up the number of "likes" on a business page, I still believe it is essential to set one up separate from your personal account. I have seen many people start out using their personal Facebook account for their online content, only to reach the maximum number of "friends" allowed eventually. They then had to scramble to create a business page and encourage everyone to "like" it. Facebook users are more accustomed to "friending" people than "liking" pages, so it does take longer to build a business page than a friend list.

To set up a Facebook business page, simply visit **facebook.com/about/pages.** You will need to log into your personal Facebook account first, and then the system will walk you through the steps necessary to create your business page. Creating a Facebook business page is free and easy to do, and I consider it an essential step in establishing your brand and building your YouTube channel.

The first decision you will need to make is to **name your business Facebook page**. My Facebook business page is *Ann Eckhart*, the same name as my books and YouTube channel, not to mention the name I use on my other social media accounts. You will want your page name to match your YouTube channel name, too.

As you go forward with creating more social media accounts, you will again want your name to be the same across all platforms. Remember, the goal is to BRAND yourself so that people will recognize you on all forms of social media. Therefore, now is the time to make sure you are happy with your channel name.

There are all kinds of things you can personalize on your Facebook page. You want to add a profile picture and a banner. I have a headshot as my profile picture, and I make my own customized banners for social media on apps like Canva and WordSwag. Whatever photos or graphics you choose, remember that this is your BUSINESS page, so keep it professional. You do not want to post potentially controversial photographs of yourself; look at other YouTube creators Facebook pages to get an idea of the kinds of photos and graphics that are acceptable to share.

You will also want to fill out the extensive **About** section of your page to provide people with information about your YouTube channel. However, since this is your BUSINESS page and separate from your personal page, you will want to be careful with how much information you share. While you may have your cell phone number available on your personal page to keep in touch with family and friends, unless you have a brick-and-mortar location that you want people to call, you will want to leave that section blank on your business page.

You will first need to choose the **Category** for your page; as a YouTube creator, there are several categories you can choose from, such as "Public Figure," "Entertainer," or "Personal Blog or Website." I prefer the latter; please do not dub yourself as a public figure or celebrity until you have reached at least a million subscribers. Touting yourself as something other than you are will turn off potential followers. "Entertainer" or "Entertainment" are less offensive than "Public Figure," in my opinion.

You will need to select a sub-category for your Facebook page, too. And do not worry about being locked into your selections; you can easily change them at any time. In fact, Facebook regularly updates the options, so it is always good to check them a couple of times a year to see if better selections have been added.

In addition to your **Name** (the name of your page, i.e., your YouTube channel name), you can edit your Facebook URL so that it ends in that name. This provides you with a clickable URL link that you will want to provide on both your YouTube channel "About" section as well as in the description box under all of your videos. The URL for my Facebook page is facebook.com/anneckhart.

Once you have created your Facebook business page, you will be able to fill in the **About** section. Here you can enter in your **Location**, although I keep this field blank to protect my privacy. Next up are **two description fields,** one short and one long. I have one simple sentence in the first field (Ann Eckhart is an author, YouTube content creator, and Ebay seller based in Iowa.). I provide a bit more information in the second field (*Welcome to the official Facebook page of Ann Eckhart (formerly SeeAnnSave)! I am an author, vlogger, influencer, and Ebayer. I am also a pug dog mom, caregiver, and Walt Disney World fanatic!*). Again, you can edit these fields at any time, so do not worry about being locked into what you first type in.

Next, you will see **your page's statistics**, including how many people "like" your page and how many people "follow" the page. Underneath these numbers will be a **field to enter one website URL.** If you create your Facebook page specifically to promote your YouTube channel, you will want to put your channel URL into this field. I have my Amazon Author Page linked here, but regardless, you will be able to further link your other sites down on the page.

In the next section, you can enter a **phone number**; however, you should leave this field blank unless you want strangers to call you. There are also fields for you to post your **email address** (I have a business email that I share across all of my accounts; I just use the one that I set up in Google when I started my YouTube channel), **additional categories** (these are Facebook's versions of "tags"; I chose "writer," "author," and "video creator"); and finally, there is space to post **all of your other**

links (I have links to my Instagram, Twitter, and Pinterest pages as well as both of my YouTube channels here).

You will also want to take some time to customize your page's **Settings**, the link for which can be found on the left side of your page. There are lots of options available for you to edit here; I am going to share with you what mine are and why I chose them

- **Page Visibility:** Page published (obviously as my page is public on Facebook!)
- **Visitor Posts:** Disable posts by other people on the page (I chose this setting to prevent anyone from sharing their posts on my page; this is mainly done to control spam and trolls.)
- **Post and Story Sharing:** Allow Sharing To Stories (This allows my followers to share my posts with their Facebook friends, which can help me gain more followers and/or clicks through to my Amazon Author Page and YouTube channels.)
- **Audience Optimization for Posts** (I personally left this blank)
- **Messages:** I do not allow people to contact my Page privately by showing them the Messaging buttons. This is a personal decision; if you feel comfortable having your followers message you through Facebook, then you can select this option.
- **Tagging Ability:** I do not allow others to tag photos and videos published by my page to maintain control over my content.
- **Others Tagging This Page:** I do not allow these options for the same reason of maintaining control over my content.
- **Country Restriction:** I have none selected.
- **Age Restrictions:** I chose Public, but there are also options for ages 17 and up, 18 and up, 19 and up, 21 and up, and Alcohol-Related.
- **Page Moderation:** I left this field blank, but you can block posts or comments that contain specific words.
- **Profanity Filter:** I have this turned Off, but you can also select from Medium or Strong.

- **Similar Page Suggestions:** I selected for my page to be included when recommending similar Facebook Pages that people might like on a Page timeline.
- **Page Updates:** I selected to publish posts when info is uploaded on my page automatically.
- **Post in Multiple Languages:** I have this turned off as I only know English!
- **Translate Automatically:** However, I have selected Facebook to show people who understand other languages' automatic translations of my posts when available.
- **Comment Ranking:** I chose for Facebook to show me the most relevant comments by default.
- **Content Distribution:** I have not chosen to prohibit downloading to Facebook.

Finally, there are options to **Download Page** and **Merge Page**, providing you with links to complete those tasks if you so desire (I have never used these). And the last option is to **Remove Page**, which will delete your page so that nobody will see it or find it. If you ever select to delete your page, you will have 14 days to restore it if you change your mind.

Once you have your Facebook business page set up, it is time to start building your audience by getting people to "Like" your page. You will be able to invite friends and family on your personal page to "Like" your new business page. And of course, you can promote your Facebook page on your YouTube channel by adding your page URL to the "About" section on YouTube as well as providing the link under all of your videos.

Once you have a Facebook page and other social media accounts, you will want to make sure to provide links to all your pages in the "About" information section of your YouTube channel home page, plus in the description box under each video. Note that you need to enter the full URL address of your sites, including the "http://" as only the complete "http" links will be active, allowing viewers to click through to the sites directly.

To make this process easy, I have my full description bar write-up and links in a Word document that I simply copy and paste into the description box of every video I upload. I will discuss this further in *Chapter Nine: A Day in the Life.*

As I mentioned earlier, I make sure all of my social networking accounts and websites work together to drive as much traffic as possible to my videos. When I upload a new YouTube video, I post the link to Facebook. Unfortunately, Facebook has made it increasingly difficult for people to see posts, hiding posts from business pages as they want those of us with pages to pay for the posts to be seen. This is frustrating, but there are some things you can do to help your posts be seen.

Once you have a business page and start posting there, you will likely notice the **Boost** buttons under posts that encourage you to pay for your updates to be directly shown to your followers. And while it can be tempting to spend $5 or more to ensure your posts are seen, resist the urge to boost everything you put on Facebook as the results are not worth the cost. Instead, perhaps spend $5 every other week or so to promote one post to see if it affects your page "likes" and/or your YouTube subscriber growth.

I personally choose one video per week to "boost" on Facebook, typically one that is already performing well. You might be wondering why I would focus on a video that is already getting views. The reason is "low hanging fruit." It is better to promote your best-selling products, in this case, a video that is performing well, in the hopes that it will bring people to your other products, in this case, the other videos on your channel.

I utilize this technique when I run ads for my books. I only advertise my best sellers. These books sell well without advertising, but sales on all of my books increase when I advertise them. Why? Because if someone buys one of my books and enjoys it, they are likely to come back and purchase another of my titles. And since my best sellers are my best-reviewed, I want to start them off with my best books.

The same is true for running ads to a well-performing YouTube video. If a lot of people are organically finding and watching a particular video, it only makes sense that others will join in once they see it is popular.

Think about it like this: Say you saw an ad for a product with no reviews. Amazon products will show the number of stars a product has received, which is a good indicator of how popular an item is. You may get an ad for a product with no reviews, but then you get an ad for a product with thousands of reviews. When choosing between the two, most people will go with the product with the most reviews.

In the same way, on YouTube, viewers go with the videos with the most views. Let's say you do a search for "best vlogging camera" on YouTube. The results show you a variety of videos that all look relatively the same. The only difference is the number of views they have. If you must choose one, will you watch the video with only a few dozen views or the video with thousands of views? I am betting that you choose the one that the most people have watched.

If you have a video that is performing well on YouTube, that is the one I would choose to "boost" on Facebook. Boosting a post turns your post into an ad that will be shown to the audience you specify. Facebook can target your ad to who they think will be the most interested in it, or you can narrow down your audience.

When I boost a post that features a YouTube video, I choose for Facebook to target the people who "like" my page AND the people who are connected to them (the friends and family of the people who already "like" my page). You have likely seen ads in your Facebook feed and have noticed that the ad shows you which of your Facebook friends like that company. Seeing that your friends already like a company will make you more likely to click on the ad.

However, if you are new in your YouTube journey, you likely have very few people who "like" your page. In this case, I would recommend that you let Facebok choose the audience they will show the ad to. You can set a low budget – like I said, even just $5 – for a few days and see how it performs.

Because Facebook is selective about what posts they will show your followers, it is essential to do more than just post links to your Facebook page to engage your audience. Facebook prefers original posts and photos over links that you simply copy and paste to your page. I try to post a regular status update at least once a day, which is more likely to be shown to my followers than a post with a link that I share directly from my blog. I also occasionally share photos on my Facebook page; like status updates, pictures tend to show up to more people than just links to my blog. Since my Facebook and Instagram accounts are linked, it is easy to share whatever I post to Instagram to Facebook. That way, I can knock out two social media posts in just one step.

Another way to engage your Facebook page users is to post "teasers" for upcoming videos. Post a photo of yourself as you are prepping to film, or a picture of something you are getting ready to share, with the message that a new video will be coming the next day. This will get people excited about your latest video to be released.

You want to encourage people to "like" and "comment" on your Facebook posts in the hopes their activity will show up on their friends' feeds, which will help more people come to your page. As I mentioned for Facebook ads, you have likely seen this happen on your Facebook feed, where it will show you that a friend liked a post or a page. The convenient "like" thumbs up icon will be there, making it easy for you, too, to "like" the page.

It is always my hope that when someone "likes" one of my posts that their friends will see it, check out my page, and then "like" it, too. As I mentioned earlier, Facebook shows status updates and photos more than links; so, I get more "likes" and comments on my status updates and pictures than I do when I simply share links to my blog posts or videos.

Also, as I mentioned earlier, you may decide that a Facebook page can act like your blog or website rather than setting up a separate site. Many YouTube creators do not have a blog or website, preferring to use Facebook as their homepage. So, unless you have the time to devote to maintaining a separate website, consider just using Facebook along with other social networking sites to promote your YouTube channel. I recommend you do Facebook FIRST, as you can always add a blog/website later in your journey.

Another Facebook option is to form a private group. This is again something that you will want to consider when you have more followers. But a private group where you can interact with your viewers is a popular way to engage your audience.

As I discussed earlier in the book, I used to have a blog called SeeAnnSave, where I shared free samples, coupons, and clearance deals. I also used to put a lot of that type of money-saving content on YouTube. When I closed my blog, I heard from so many readers who really missed it. So, I created a private Facebook group where I now post the deals that I used to share on my blog.

You can do the same with your YouTube videos, posting videos in a private group before they go live, answering viewer questions, and holding giveaways. Anything you can do to create "brand" loyalty is always a good idea, and Facebook makes that easy and free!

TWITTER: If you do not already have a Twitter account, you can create one at **Twitter.com.** If you do have an account that you are active on, consider creating a new one just for your YouTube channel. As with Facebook, you want to keep your personal and business lives separate on Twitter. Make sure your Twitter handle is the same as your YouTube channel. Remember, part of branding is being known as ONE name across ALL social media platforms. You will need a different email address for each Twitter account you create; since you were given a Gmail address when you signed up for a Google account and YouTube channel, you can use that one.

Like Facebook, Twitter provides a free and easy way to connect with viewers and drive traffic to your YouTube videos. YouTube makes sharing your videos to Twitter super easy as there is a Twitter share button under all videos. Simply click on the Twitter icon and link your YouTube account to your Twitter account to share the title of your video, as well as the direct link and the thumbnail of your video.

Twitter allows users to share posts of 280 characters or less. While your video's title and the link along with the thumbnail will automatically be put into the Twitter field, you can increase your exposure by adding hashtags. **Hashtags** are simply keywords that follow a pound (#) sign. For instance, when I film a video about selling on Ebay, I will use hashtags such as:

- #ebay
- #ebayseller
- #reselling
- #makingmoneyonline
- #homebasedbusiness
- #youtube
- #video

I try to add as many hashtags as I have room for as savvy Twitter users search for tweets using hashtags, which increases the chance of you driving traffic to your videos.

When you share a YouTube video to Twitter, Twitter automatically tags the official YouTube Twitter account in your tweet. Do not remove the tag as it is another free and easy way to potentially get more views as people who follow YouTube might see the tag and click to watch your video.

I set aside some time every evening to connect with other Twitter users since I can do this on my iPhone while relaxing in front of the TV. I follow other resellers and YouTube creators, retweet posts I like, reply to posts, and post a Tweet or two of my own. Twitter works best when you actively engage with other users, so it is crucial to spend some time each day networking on Twitter so that you can grow your followers.

Some Twitter users follow everyone who follows them, which can certainly be a way to build up your followers. You can also "network" with other folks on Twitter by replying to, retweeting, or favoring tweets. As I mentioned when setting up your Facebook page, you can add all your social media links, including your Twitter URL, in the "About" section of your Facebook business page; so hopefully, some of your Facebook fans will follow you to Twitter. To encourage this, about once a week, post your Twitter link directly to your Facebook page to make it easy for people to click through and "follow" you.

Add your Twitter URL to the list of other links you share on your YouTube channel, both in your channel information section as well as under each video. Remember to add the http:// to your link to make it active so that users can directly click through to your Twitter account.

The **Edit Profile** feature located on your Twitter homepage allows you to customize the look and information people will see when they click on your profile. Add a nice, clear photo of yourself (or your logo, if you have one), and add a header image. Write up a brief but fun description of yourself. Put the link to your YouTube channel in the website field so that people can click through to your videos. And finally, click on "theme colors" to customize your profile page even further.

Note that Twitter is decreasing in popularity as of late, so do not fret if you do not find yourself gaining a lot of followers. Nowadays, most people simply search for hashtags when using Twitter; they may find your post, but they are not as likely as they once were to follow you. However, the main goal is for people to click on and watch your videos. As long as your tweets are accomplishing that, do not worry if you are gaining followers or not.

Personalizing your Twitter profile, posting regularly, using hashtags, and engaging with other users every day will increase people finding your YouTube videos and subscribing to your channel, therefore earning you more AdSense revenue. And if you do end up growing a large

Twitter following, you will be able to negotiate sponsored content in your feed.

PINTEREST: Pinterest is often overlooked when it comes to promoting YouTube videos, but, as with Facebook and Twitter, it is another free and easy way to drive traffic to your channel and increase your video views. And increased views mean more AdSense dollars!

If you do not already have a Pinterest account, you can create one at **pinterest.com**. If you are already an active Pinterest user, you can just do what I have done and add a "YouTube Videos" board to your account. However, if you have a very diverse Pinterest account with content that is irrelevant to your YouTube videos, you may consider setting up a second account. My content tends to all be similar, so it is okay for me to have a "board" for my videos.

Pinterest allows you to create boards where you pin content. You can "pin" content that others have posted, and you can also share your own "pins." Pinterest started as a way for people, mainly women, to "pin" craft ideas and recipes to virtual boards. However, Pinterest is quickly becoming a tool for businesses to get the word out about their products and develop brand loyalty. And as you grow your YouTube brand, you will want to make Pinterest a part of your marketing strategy.

As I mentioned, I have a board on Pinterest that I have titled *"YouTube Videos."* As with Facebook and Twitter, YouTube provides a "share" icon for Pinterest underneath all videos. After uploading a video to YouTube, I simply click on the Pinterest icon and "pin" it to my *"YouTube Videos"* board. The video then appears on the feed of those who follow me on Pinterest. They can click through to my video directly from my pin. And if they "repin" the post, then their followers will also see it. I have noticed a dramatic increase in traffic to my books and to my YouTube channel since I started pinning my links to my books and videos to Pinterest.

Just as you should be doing with your Facebook and Twitter links, be sure to link your Pinterest page in your YouTube channel profile as well as in the description bar underneath all your videos. And put the link in the "General Information" section of your Facebook page. Be sure to periodically share your Pinterest link on both Facebook and Twitter to attract new followers.

You may be noticing by now that a big part of social networking is to have all your sites working together. Include all your social media links on your blog/website and Facebook. Post your Twitter and Pinterest links to Facebook. Share your Facebook and Pinterest links on Twitter. Ensure all of your sites are drawing traffic to each other, which will help grow your brand and your audience. The more you can get your YouTube channel link out there, the easier it will be for people to find your videos and for your channel to grow!

INSTAGRAM: Instagram offers another free, easy, and fun way to interact with your YouTube subscribers and gain more viewers. In fact, in just the past year or so, Instagram has brought my YouTube channel more traffic than Facebook, Twitter, and Pinterest combined.

To create an Instagram account, go to **Instagram.com.** Again, make sure your Instagram name is the same as your YouTube channel and other social media sites. If you already have a personal Instagram account, consider creating a second one specifically for your YouTube channel and brand.

Instagram allows you to share photos and "like" and comment on photos shared by others. While you cannot put a full-length YouTube video on Instagram, you can share content and put in links to your channel, both with your photos and in your profile.

And while you cannot add a full-length YouTube video to Instagram, you can add video there, both through **Stories** and through **Reels** as well as one-minute long **Posts.**

Instagram Stories: If you are already on Instagram, you likely know that at the top of the screen are small photos of the people you follow. When you click on a person's picture, you will see the "stories" they have posted, both photos and video. This content remains on Instagram for 24 hours before it disappears. As long as there is a colorful ring around the photo, there is content to view.

Creating your own Instagram Story is simple. Just tap on the "+" icon at the top of the screen. Here you can choose to create a regular post, i.e., one that appears in your Instagram feed. Or you can choose **Story, Reels** or **Live.** Choosing *Story* will allow you to upload a photo from your phone's camera roll or a short 15-second clip from your camera roll. Or you can create a photo or video clip right in the Instagram app by using the camera feature. This option is the large round white circle at the bottom of the page. In the same row are the various filters you can apply.

But let's focus on how to promote your YouTube channel in your stories. What I do is post the thumbnail of the video I want people to watch on my channel. Now, I have over 10,000 Instagram followers, which means I can utilize the "Swipe Up" feature. This allows me to post a direct link in my stories; when viewers "swipe up," they go directly to wherever the link leads. In this case, it would take people right to my video.

If you do not have the "Swipe Up" feature, you will need to direct followers to your YouTube channel link, which you should have in your Instagram bio. If YouTube is your only website, it should be the only link you have. You would then do what I do by posting a picture of your video's thumbnail, but instead of instructing people to "Swipe Up," you would ask them to click on the link in your bio. The standard way to do this is just to type "Link In Bio" and then tag yourself. For instance, I would type "Link In Bio @ann_eckhart," which would take them directly to my bio where my link is.

But what do you do if you have multiple links? What if you want to provide links to a website, social media accounts, and affiliate advertisers? It is easy, as you use an add-on feature called a "link tree," which allows you to create a page with multiple links that only requires one link in your profile to access.

Instagram only allows users to have ONE link in their profile. However, link trees enable multiple links. These link trees or landing pages are also used on TikTok, which also only allows one link in each bio.

There are several companies that provide link trees. Most have a basic free option with more advanced paid options. I recommend starting with a free option first, as you can always upgrade later if you feel you need to.

Some link tree/landing page options include:

Beacons: The only option that includes the ability to monetize links.

Campsite: Offers images next to the links for nice visual appeal.

ContactInBio: Considered a close second in popularity to Linktree.

Link-in Profile: Instead of text links, you can add in your own images and make them clickable. The cost is $9.99 per month or $99 a year after a one-month free trial.

Linktree: The first and arguably still the most popular of all the landing page sites.

Lnk.bio: Minimalist design but limited features in the free version.

Milkshake: Unique in that it turns your "link in bio" into a free website.

Shorby: Features unlimited links and social icons but has no free option. Plans start at $9 per month.

TapBio: Pulls all data from Instagram and YouTube to create clickable "cards."

Once you have your link situation set up and are comfortable using Instagram Stories, it is time to take it up a notch and try Instagram's newest feature: "Reels."

Instagram Reels: Reels allow you to create short videos in your feed. The difference between a *reel* and a *story* is that you can save your Reels to your main Instagram feed, which will make them accessible forever. Remember that "stories" disappear after 24-hours. Reels, however, can be permanent.

According to Instagram's instructions, here is how to create a Reel:

"**Select Reels at the bottom of the Instagram camera**. You will see a variety of creative editing tools on the left side of your screen to help create your Reel, including:

- **Audio:** Search for a song from the Instagram music library. You can also use your own original audio by simply recording a Reel with it. When you share a Reel with original audio, your audio will be attributed to you, and if you have a public account, people can create Reels with your audio by selecting "Use Audio" from your Reel.
- **AR Effects:** Select one of the many effects in our effect gallery, created both by Instagram and creators all over the world, to record multiple clips with different effects.
- **Timer and Countdown:** Set the timer to record any of your clips hands-free. Once you press record, you will see a 3-2-1 countdown before recording begins for the amount of time you selected.
- **Align:** Line up objects from your previous clip before recording your next to help create seamless transitions for moments like outfit changes or adding new friends into your Reel.
- **Speed:** Choose to speed up or slow down part of the video or audio you selected. This can help you stay on a beat or make slow-motion videos.

Reels can be recorded in a series of clips (one at a time), all at once, or using video uploads from your gallery. Record the first clip by pressing and holding the capture button. You will see a progress indicator at the top of the screen as you record. Stop recording to end each clip."

Instagram offers the following instruction for sharing Reels:

"*With Reels, you can share with your followers, and they can be discovered by the vast, diverse Instagram community on Explore.*

If you have a Public Account: *You can share your Reel to a dedicated space in Explore, where it has the chance to be seen and discovered by the* *wider Instagram community. You can also share your Reel with your followers by posting it to your Feed. When you share Reels featuring certain songs, hashtags, or effects, your Reel may also appear on dedicated pages when someone clicks on that song, hashtag, or effect.*

If you have a Private Account: Reels follows your privacy settings on Instagram. You can share to Feed so only your followers can see your Reel. People will not be able to use original audio from your Reels, and people cannot share your Reels with others who do not follow you.

Once your Reel is ready, move to the share screen, where you can save a draft of your Reel, change the cover image, add a caption and hashtags, and tag your friends. After you share your Reel, it will live on a separate Reels tab on your profile, where people can find the Reels you have shared. If you also share to your Feed, your Reel will appear on your primary profile grid, though you have the option to remove it.

Whether you have a public or private account, you can share your Reel to your Story, close friends, or in a direct message. If you do so, your Reel will behave like a regular Story — it will not be shared to Reels in Explore, it will not appear on your profile, and it will disappear after 24 hours."

Finally, in addition to your regular *Feed, Stories,* and *Reels,* Instagram also offers a **Live** option, and the recently added a **Live Room** feature, which allows you to live stream with up to three other people. Here are Instagram's instructions for Live Rooms:

"Instagram Live: To start a Live Room, swipe left and pick the Live camera option. Then, add a title and tap the Rooms icon to add your guests. You will see people who have requested to go live with you, and you can also search for a guest to add. When you start a Live Room, you will remain at the top of the screen when you add guests.

As a broadcaster, you can add up to three guests at once or one by one (for example, you could start with two guests, and add a surprise guest as the third participant later). Going live with multiple guests is a great way to increase your reach, as guests' followers can also be notified."

Note that you do not have to do a "Live Room" you can go live independently if you prefer. Regardless, the great thing about going live on

Instagram is that you can now earn money from these videos. On May 27, 2020, Instagram announced the following:

"Creators have always been at the core of our community. Since the earliest days of Instagram, they have inspired people around the world with their talents, shared their lives, and built their personal brands from the ground up.

We have always been committed to supporting creators as they turn their passion into livelihoods; because every creator is unique, that means providing a mix of monetization tools to help creators of all sizes, from the emerging to the more established. Today we are announcing new ways for creators to make money through Instagram Live and IGTV.

Introducing Badges in Live: *During the COVID-19 crisis, we have seen people supporting their favorite creators in Live with comments, likes, and donations. To give fans another way to participate and show their love, we are introducing badges that viewers can purchase during a live video.*

In recent months, we have seen creators embrace Live in new ways, leading to a 70% increase in views from February to March. From fitness instructors to dancers, artists to chefs, Live has helped creators and businesses stay connected to their followers and bring people together. With badges, creators can generate income from the content they are already creating.

Badges will appear next to a person's name throughout the live video. Fans who have purchased badges in Live will stand out in the comments and unlock additional features, including placement on a creator's list of badge holders and access to a special heart."

Instagram Badges are available for viewers to purchase for 99-cents, $1.99, or three for $4.99. In essence, they function like a "tip jar" for viewers to "tip" creators. Right now, *Badges* are only available to certain accounts; you will be notified by Instagram if you are eligible.

Of the three options - *Stories, Reels,* and *Live* - I only use *Stories.* To be honest, it is more important for me to get people to watch my YouTube videos because the payout is higher on YouTube versus Instagram. While some creators are making money with *Badges*, it is nowhere near what people are earning on YouTube, at least not yet. As long as you have ads enabled on your YouTube videos, you WILL earn a cut of AdSense revenue. However, there is no guarantee that anyone who watches one of your live Instagram videos will "tip" you.

However, it is still beneficial to learn all of the features a site offers, so definitely test out the *Reels* and *Live* Instagram options, so you at least know how they work should you want to use them in the future. Instagram is continually rolling out new features as they compete with the other social media networks, so staying up-to-date with their offerings is important.

The best use of Instagram that I have found is to connect with subscribers on a more personal level. While I talk a lot about business on YouTube, on Instagram, I share personal photos of my dogs, family, and life. I also post pictures of fun activities such as eating dinner out (Instagram users love food photos!) or attending local events. And I also post funny memes and jokes, which are always a hit and increase engagement.

Whatever my Instagram content, however, the main goal is to further connect with followers who are interested in the content I am providing, whether it is on my YouTube channels or in the books I write.

Just like on Twitter, **hashtags** are a big part of getting your content on Instagram found. I like to include three to five hashtags with every photo I share. If I share a picture of a subscription box I have reviewed on YouTube, I might use hashtags such as:

- #subscriptionbox
- #unboxing
- #review
- #youtube
- #youtuber

TIP: You can create a long list of hashtags in the "notes" app on your phone and simply copy and paste them onto all of your Instagram posts. The goal of these hashtags is for the many Instagram users who search for specific hashtags to find yours, so using as many as possible increases your chances of being found. You can also put the hashtags in your Instagram *Stories*; however, I typically only add a couple there because the hashtags literally take up space on the screen and can distract from the post itself.

Hashtags bring non-followers to my posts all the time. And not all of them end up following me. However, even if they do not follow me on Instagram, they may still check out my profile and click through to my Amazon Author Page or my YouTube channel. And again, driving traffic to the things I am earning money from is my ultimate goal.

When promoting my YouTube channel via Instagram, I post a thumbnail from my most recent video and encourage followers to head over to my channel to watch it. Since the link to my YouTube channel is in my Linktree menu, which is linked in my bio, I usually write: *"New video now live on my YouTube channel; direct link in my profile @ann_eckhart."* The "@" link will take users to my profile page, where the active link to my Linktree menu, and therefore my YouTube channel, will be. Then the user simply clicks on my YouTube channel URL, taking them straight to my videos.

As I mentioned, once you reach 10,000 Instagram followers, you can add "swipe up" links to your Instagram stories. After I share about a new video on my main Instagram feed, I also post about it in my Instagram stories with a direct link to the video so that people can "swipe up" to watch it. I usually add a fun GIF swipe-up graphic along with a song from Instagram's music list. I have found that using the "swipe up" feature to take people directly to my YouTube videos is the most valuable part of reaching 10,000 Instagram followers.

As with Twitter and Pinterest, it is a good idea to actively network with others on Instagram by following them back, "liking" their pictures, and leaving comments. I like to spend about 10 minutes a day scrolling through my Instagram feed to check out what others are posting and engage with my favorite posts.

Note, also, that Instagram is an app. While you can see your Instagram feed, edit your profile, and add followers on a computer, you can only add your own posts using the app on your smartphone or tablet. Unlike Facebook and Twitter, which both work about the same on a cell phone or desktop computer, Instagram works best on mobile devices.

TIKTOK: TikTok is the new social media network on the scene, and it has really taken off since it launched in 2018. In just a few short years, TikTok has amassed over 100 million users, making it arguably the fastest growing social media site online.

TikTok is an app-based, short-form, video-sharing platform that allows users to create video clips anywhere from 15 seconds to three minutes long. Initially, TikTok was used mainly by those sharing music and dance; however, now, it is popular with nearly every demographic with a wide range of topics. From cooking and fashion to gossip and vlogging, TikTok now attracts celebrities alongside everyday folks who, even if they do not upload their own content, love to scroll through the feed.

So how can you use TikTok to drive traffic to your YouTube channel? Any way you want to! Whether you want to pop on to let your followers know that a new video has gone live or want to share a clip of a recent video, it is up to you. Those who successfully utilize the site to grow their businesses are posting at least once a day on TikTok, so setting up a schedule will help you be consistent.

I like to share my recent Ebay sales on my TikTok feed. Not only does this drive traffic to my books, but it also gets people interested in my YouTube videos, as many of them are reseller-related.

Just like Instagram, TikTok allows only one link in a creator's profile. If you want to put more links in, you can use the same link tree/landpage plug-ins that I laid out earlier in this book. Fortunately, TikTok allows users to link their Instagram and YouTube channels in their bios and provides the icons for each site. This frees up your primary link to add in a link to your website or Facebook page. I personally have my Amazon Author Page as my link, and then I link Instagram and YouTube with TikTok's interface.

NETWORK WITH FELLOW YOUTUBERS: There is a fine line between networking with other YouTube creators to grow your channel and outright using them to help you. One of the most painful things I see new YouTubers do is BEGGING people to subscribe to their channel. They stalk the successful YouTube channels and leave comments asking the viewers of someone else's channel to sub their channel, too. Or worse, they send out private messages to the subscribers of other channels asking them to subscribe.

If you are creating quality content, there is no reason to beg for subscribers. In fact, it is so tacky and frowned upon nowadays that you will likely turn off potential viewers. However, there are ways that you can network with other YouTube creators that are beneficial for both you and them.

First, you want to SUPPORT other channels. Subscribe to the channels you actually like, give their videos a thumbs up, leave nice comments, and share their videos via your social networks (I like to share my favorite videos to both Twitter and Pinterest using the "share" buttons located under each video).

Showing your support to other channels not only helps your favorite YouTube creators, but it will likely get you noticed by their subscribers, drawing people to your channel. Again, do these things because you want to support channels that you enjoy; you should help other creators without expecting that they will return the favor, especially if the channels are much larger than yours.

Suppose you develop a friendly "relationship" with another YouTuber (they are replying to your comments or noticing your Tweets). In that case, it is okay to casually mention that you also make videos similar to theirs. But do so without the expectation that you will get anything back from them. It is best to let these relationships develop naturally; just like in real life, genuine internet friendships are based on both parties having an equal amount of respect and admiration for one another.

Suppose you find another YouTube creator with the same number of subscribers as you have and who is creating similar content. In that case, you may want to suggest doing a collaboration video with them. Many YouTubers do "collabs," where they partner with another channel to create videos with similar themes.

Video collab ideas include sending each other boxes of goodies to open on camera, answering "tag" questions, or participating in group challenges. If you live in the same area, have gotten to know another creator well, and feel safe meeting them in person, you can even film videos together, posting a video to your respective channels and then directing viewers to go to the other channel to watch the other video. For instance, I have seen several resellers get together to shop at flea markets or antique malls. They each "vlog" their experiences and post to their channels, encouraging their viewers to check out the other respective vlogs.

Collaboration videos help you make friends in the YouTube community; everyone benefits by encouraging viewers to check out all the participating channels. People who do collab videos link each other's channels in their video's description boxes, and the videos are then shared via everyone's respective social media accounts.

Create great content, support the channels you enjoy watching, utilize your social media accounts, and let the viewers and subscribers build naturally! After all, you want people to WATCH your videos, not just hit subscribe because they have been paid or guilted into doing so.

MOST SUBSCRIBED TO YOUTUBE CHANNELS

1. T-Series with 186 million subscribers (Indian music record label)
2. Cocomelon with 113 million subscribers (children's 3D animation videos)
3. PewDiePie with 110 million subscribers (Swedish gaming and comedy personality)
4. SET India with 108 million subscribers (Hindi-language entertainment channel)

5. Kids Diana Show with 80.4 million subscribers (Ukrainian children's channel)

6. WWE with 78.7 million subscribers (American professional wrestling)

7. Like Nastya with 74.9 million subscribers (Russian children's channel)

8. Zee Music Company with 74.4 million subscribers (Indian music company)

9. 5-Minute Crafts with 72.8 million subscribers (crafting and life hacks)

10. Vlad and Niki with 69.3 million subscribers (Russian children's channel)

11. Canal KondZilla with 64.4 million subscribers (Brazilian entertainment channel)

12. MrBeast with 64.2 million subscribers (stunts)

13. Justin Bieber with 64 million subscribers (Canadian singer)

14. Blackpink with 62.5 million subscribers (Korean female pop group)

15. Zee TV with 58.1 million subscribers (India entertainment programming)

16. HYBE LABELS with 57.9 million subscribers (South Korean entertainment label)

17. Dude Perfect with 56.3 million subscribers (American sports and comedy)

18. Marshmello with 53.2 million subscribers (American electronic music DJ)

19. Shemaroo Filmi Gaane with 53.1 million subscribers (India movie distributor)

20. Movieclips with 53 million subscribers (film clips and trailers)

21. Sony SAB with 53 million subscribers (Indian comedy)

22. Bangtan TV with 52.8 million subscribers (South Korean boy band)

23. Pinkfong! Kids Stories & Songs with 50 million subscribers (South Korean children's channel)
24. ChuChu TV Nursery Rhymes & Kids Songs with 49.4 million subscribers (Indian children's programming)
25. Ariana Grande with 48.7 million subscribers (American pop singer)

CHAPTER EIGHT:

BEST PRACTICES

Great equipment, film quality, and marketing are not enough when it comes to gaining viewers and subscribers on YouTube. Follow these best practices to ensure your YouTube career is a success.

PAYING FOR SUBSCRIBERS: One thing you absolutely do NOT want to do is pay for people to subscribe to your YouTube channel. There are online companies that, for a price, will get people (usually automated computer "robots" or "bots") to subscribe to your channel. However, VIEWS are what create AdSense revenue, not subscribers. People who have been paid to subscribe to a channel will not actually watch the videos. Plus, some sites track YouTube channel subscribers, views, and revenue and post the results online; so, it is obvious when someone has paid for subscribers as there will be a sudden massive spike in their numbers. It can actually hurt your channel if you have a large number of subscribers but a low number of video views in comparison.

CHANNEL DESIGN: When you log into YouTube, you can select **Your Channel** (click on your profile picture in the top left-hand corner, and it is the first option in the drop-down menu) to edit the design of your channel's homepage via the **Customize Channel** icon. Once on the Channel customization page, there are three sections you can work on: Layout, Branding, and Basic Info.

Under the **Layout** tab, you can add a **Channel trailer for people who haven't yet subscribed to your channel.** This acts as a commercial or preview for anyone who comes to your channel but is not yet subscribed. You can also upload a **Featured video for returning subscribers** to give a special welcome back for your loyal viewers.

Under the **Branding** tab, you can change your **Profile picture**, which is the photo that appears on not just your channel page but also next to all of your videos and next to any comments you post on your videos or anyone else's. A Banner image appears across the top of your channel. You need to provide an image that measures 2048x1152 pixels and 6MB or less. There are a lot of free apps that can create these specialty images; I personally use a YouTube thumbnail app that offers multiple sizes for social media graphics.

Finally, you can add a **Video watermark** that will appear on your videos in the video player's right-hand corner. An image that measures 150x150 pixels is recommended. The image must be a PNG, GIF (no animations), BMP, or JPEG file that is 1MB or less. My watermark is my YouTube channel logo.

Under the **Basic info** tab is where you can add all of the links to your social media accounts, along with a blog/website if you have one. First, there is a field to write your channel's description, which is under **About.**

On my main "Ann Eckhart" channel, my *About* section currently reads: *Hi, and welcome to my channel! My name is Ann, and on this channel, I feature dedicated sit-down videos, including hauls, reviews, and unboxings. If you love subscription boxes and shopping hauls, you are in the right place! :-)*

On my second channel, "Ann Eckhart Vlog," my *About* section currently reads: *Welcome to my vlog channel! Some of you may know me from my main channel, Ann Eckhart, where I post dedicated sit-down videos. This channel is for my vlogs, most of which revolve around making money from home as a self-employed author, reseller, and online content creator. I also share more fun and personal content, including my pug dogs and life in Iowa.*

In both *About* sections, I also provide my business email address, although I specify that it is for business inquiries only, such as sponsorship and brand deal proposals. I had to include that warning to stop people from sending me personal emails; I was getting so many messages a day that it took away from my ability to get any work done. It is one of those "tough love" moves that you will find yourself having to make as your YouTube channel grows.

In addition to my email, I also include my P.O. Box address for both PR and viewer mail. Having a P.O. Box is another decision you will want to make if you plan to build your YouTube channel, as you do not want to give out your home address to your viewers. You can get a P.O. Box from your local Post Office or UPS Store. Note that the boxes at USP Stores are considerably more than the regular postal boxes. I currently pay around $100 a year for my USPS P.O. Box.

In the middle of the "About" page is the **Links** section. Here is where you can add all of your other links. I currently have the following URLs linked: my Amazon store (this is where I have my books as well as a list of reselling supplies and household favorites), Facebook page, Twitter account, Instagram page, Pinterest board, and second YouTube channel.

The last two sections of the page are **Links on banner**, where you can choose one of your links actually to appear on your channel's banner, and **Contact info**, where you can again provide your email address. Since my main channel focuses on unboxings and reviews, I like to have my email linked twice for ease of contact from brands.

DESCRIPTION BOX: When you upload a video to YouTube, you need to create a title and put some information into the description box that is below each video. I will share what is in my description box in the next chapter of this book, "A Day in the Life." Your description box should give your viewers directions for what you want them to do, and the first thing should be the most important as it is the only one viewers will initially see unless they expand the view to reveal everything written in the box.

Some YouTubers ask viewers to give their videos a thumbs-up, leave a comment, and subscribe as the first things in their description boxes. Since I am trying to drive traffic to my books, I list my Amazon Author

Page first. Under that, I have all the links to my social networking sites, a bit about me, and my disclaimer. If I end my video by directing people to my social networking sites, I tell them that all my links are listed in the description box below and that they just must click on the down arrow to bring everything into view.

I keep the verbiage in the description box of my videos in a Word document to simply copy/paste the information whenever I upload a new video. Because viewers only see the first three lines of the description bar unless they click to expand it, it is vital to put your most crucial directive there. Make sure any websites you link have the complete URL addresses so that they will be "live," i.e., so viewers can click on them and be taken directly to your site.

ENCOURAGING LIKES, COMMENTS, and SUBSCRIPTIONS: While it may seem logical that people who watch and enjoy your videos will give them a "thumbs up," leave comments, and subscribe to your channel, most viewers will not give you any sort of feedback whatsoever. As I mentioned earlier, many people will find your videos through internet searches or by YouTube recommending your videos to them while watching another creator's channel. Most viewers do not even have YouTube accounts, so while they can watch videos via the app or on their computers, they cannot respond to your videos in any way.

For viewers who do have a YouTube account, however, you want to encourage interaction as much as possible. YouTube offers those with a YouTube account the ability to "like" (i.e., click on the little "thumbs up" icon) videos; "dislike" (i.e., click on the small "thumbs down" icon), leave a comment on videos; subscribe to channels; add videos to a "favorites" list; and share videos to their social media accounts. Encouraging people to do any of the above helps to promote your videos as the friends and followers of those viewers will see their activity and possibly decided to subscribe to your channel, too.

At the end of most of my videos, I will ask people to leave me any questions or comments they might have. I will also ask that if they liked the video, to "give it a thumbs-up." Finally, I suggest that they subscribe for more videos if they have not already done so. Some YouTube creators ask for likes and subscribers at the beginning of their videos, and some even mention it in the middle. What you do is up to you; you can always play around with this to see what feels the most natural.

MONITORING COMMENTS: Having viewers leave comments on your videos is something every YouTuber appreciates...unless those comments are mean. While most comments on my videos are positive, a "hater" comes along and says something rude or nasty every now and again. The more views a video gets, the more likely it is that someone will eventually leave a negative comment on it. The large YouTube channels whose videos get millions of views have to deal with an enormous amount of hate or "trolls," some of it so bad that it has driven successful YouTubers off the site.

Some YouTuber creators do not monitor the comments left on their videos, believing that free speech protects those who leave comments and also feeling that any comment, good or bad, is engagement that ultimately benefits their growth. While I am all for free speech, I believe it comes with consequences. And the result for someone leaving a negative comment on one of my videos is that I remove the comment and ban the person from my channel so that they cannot interact with me on YouTube in any way (either by giving a video a thumbs down, leaving me a comment, or sending me a message). My YouTube channel is my personal space. I would not allow someone to come into my home and treat me poorly, so I will not let them be mean to me through YouTube.

Even if you do not get rude comments, you will likely get the occasional "thumbs down." I am currently averaging about five dislikes on all my videos; I honestly think they are from people who subscribe to my channel so that they hit that "thumbs down" icon on my videos when they go live! While it is never a good feeling to see a dislike, realize that almost every person who makes YouTube videos gets them, and the more views a video gets, the more dislikes it will have. This is just the nature of YouTube, so try to accept it and move on, focusing on the likes and positive comments you do receive.

As I said, however, most people who leave comments are kind and supportive. I try my best to reply to anyone who leaves a comment on any of my videos, although I usually only do this for the first day or two after the video goes live. Even if I cannot leave a written reply, I try to give nice comments a "thumbs up" and click on the little heart icon next to their comment to let them know that I saw it. While YouTube used to send a message to you every time a new comment was left on one of your videos, they no longer do this. You do get a notification of activity on your videos whenever you log in (there will be a little red box next to the bell icon at the top of the page with the number of activities – likes, comments, shares, subscriptions – that are new). Still, it is now a lot harder to find and reply to comments, especially on older videos.

What I like to do is go to my **YouTube Studio** (click on your profile picture in the top right-hand corner of the page; it is the third selection in the drop-down menu). This takes me to my **Channel dashboard**, and on the left-hand side of the page are several options I can choose from, including **Comments**. Once I click on the comment icon (which is a speech bubble), I am brought to a dedicated page where comments are listed in chronological order, which allows me to see the most recent comments that have been left. It is easy for me to reply or like the comments, delete any that are inappropriate, and check on those marked **Held for review** or **Likely spam**.

Often people will continue to leave comments on videos months or even years after they were first put up, and responding to those can be nearly impossible unless you go to the dedicated Comments page so that you can see the most recent comments that have been left. Do the best you can to reply to comments, or at least to acknowledge that you are reading all comments in your videos.

You want to continually let your audience know that you appreciate all their "likes" and comments. However, the most successful YouTube channels do eventually have to stop reading and replying to comments as it is too time-consuming. At most, I may get 50 comments on a video, but it is usually much less, so it is still manageable for me. It is a great goal to have a video eventually have so many viewers and comments that you cannot keep up replying to them!

PRIVACY: When the internet first became available, people could hide anonymously behind their computers, posting whatever they wanted under screen names without anyone knowing who or where they were. However, social media, and especially YouTube, has changed that. Even if you decide to make videos where you do not appear on the screen, you will still expose yourself to the world. Therefore, it is important to take the proper safety and security measures.

Keep the exact location of your home to yourself. I only ever say that I live in Iowa; I do not mention the precise city. I do not show the front of my house. I have a P.O. Box set up for mail so that I do not have to give out my home address. I do not announce if I am going on vacation, not only so that people do not know I am not home but also not know where I will be.

Now, I am a small-time YouTuber, and these measures may seem extreme. However, it is the level of privacy that I am most comfortable with. I would rather be safe than sorry. Once you have exposed the city you live in or shown the front of your house, that information is online forever. Be extra careful when you are filming and even talking so that you do not give away too much of your privacy.

SCHEDULE & CONSISTENCY: If you are on YouTube to make money and build your brand, you will want to keep a consistent schedule of uploading videos. Some people upload on a specific day of the week, while others aim for a set number of videos per week. I typically like to post on my vlog channel on Monday, Wednesday, and Friday. For my main channel, I will post on the days when I do not have a vlog on the second channel to avoid releasing two videos on the same day. I also try to post at the same time on both channels, just to create consistency.

No matter what my posting plans are, though, I try to keep my viewers updated as to my schedule. If viewers expect a video, but something has come up, and I cannot upload, I will try to post an update. I can do this directly on YouTube by posting on the Community tab of my channel, which will show up in my subscriber's feed. And I can also post about the schedule change on Facebook, Twitter, and Instagram. Viewers will forgive an interruption in your upload schedule as long as you keep them informed.

Nothing is worse than subscribing to a new YouTube channel that promises frequent videos, only never to see them again. If you are going to be successful on YouTube, you MUST commit to it. You cannot upload a few videos, abandon your channel, and then wonder why you do not have any subscribers and are not making any money. Find a filming schedule that works for you and stick to it, at least when you are first starting out.

I recommend starting out with one or two videos a week and building on that schedule if you want to. The biggest mistake I have seen new creators make is trying to start a daily vlogging channel only to get burned out and abandon their YouTube career altogether. You can always build on your posting schedule, but it is tough to cut back on it as once viewers expect videos at specific days and times, they become agitated if you take content away.

YouTube analytics and viewers prefer videos that are around 15 minutes in length. Unless you are filming a vlog-style video or doing a live question and answer session or hangout, anything longer than 15 minutes is usually too long for most people. However, putting up videos that are too short may not satisfy viewers. And if viewers do not watch your video, you will not earn any AdSense revenue.

But of course, every situation and viewer is different. I watch channels that put up 10-minute videos and others that produce videos that are over an hour. Again, sticking to your guns and creating the content that pleases you is the most important thing, regardless of video length. Just remember that videos need to be at least 10 minutes long to insert the Mid-Roll Ad Breaks we discussed earlier in this book. To maximize your AdSense income, you will want to aim for videos that are at least 10 minutes in length so you can insert those ads.

However, more important than the length of videos is the QUALITY of them. As we discussed early on in this book, you do not need expensive camera equipment or editing software to produce quality YouTube videos (again, I film and upload videos on an iPhone). Still, you do want your videos to be clear, steady, and well-lit. Speak up so viewers can hear you. Be sure you have a nice backdrop if you are filming a sit-down video. Do your best to provide your viewers with the kind of quality video you enjoy watching.

Before you upload your video and make it live, watch it back first to ensure it looks and sounds nice. I would rather reshoot a video or skip it altogether than upload one that is of poor quality. When I upload my videos, I have them set to "Private" so that I can review them on YouTube before I make them public. And as my filming has gotten better over the years, I have deleted old videos that were not up to my standards and reshot others.

VIEWS VS. SUBSCRIBERS: Most people start on YouTube focused solely on gaining subscribers. And while the number of subscribers you have is important in your channel's overall growth and your brand, more important is the number of views your videos get.

As I touched on earlier in this chapter, I have seen people so focused on gaining subscribers that they have PAID people to subscribe to their channels. However, just because someone subscribes to your channel does not mean they will watch your videos. You only earn AdSense revenue from people WATCHING your videos, so paying for subscribers is a huge waste of time and money.

Only when someone watches your monetized videos and sees or clicks on the ads that are there will you earn any Google AdSense revenue. To attract viewers, you need to produce quality content. Not all subscribers will watch all your videos, and not all viewers will become subscribers. Suppose you have one of two videos that draw many viewers from internet searches or YouTube promoting them. In that case, you may end up making a lot of AdSense money from people just watching your videos, even if they do not end up subscribing.

However, if you are like me and you are doing YouTube for both profit AND fun, you will be consistently uploading new videos. While I have a handful of videos with current views over 100,000, as of this writing, most of my videos average about 3,000 views each within the first week, some a bit less and some a bit more. Of course, the longer my videos remain on YouTube, the more views they will get. Your videos will continue to earn AdSense money as long as people continue to watch them!

I focus on creating quality content that I am personally interested in, hoping that the viewers will respond. While I love earning AdSense, I never make a video thinking that it will make me money. I make videos that I enjoy filming and that I hope others will benefit from. Sometimes my favorite videos are the least viewed. However, I just continue making the videos I want to make, and eventually, like-minded people find them.

Making videos is a time-consuming process, so if I am not having fun, I will not do it. Viewers are smart and will see right through an attempt to film videos strictly done for views. Be yourself, have fun, and the views and subscribers will come!

DEALING WITH TROLLS: While most viewers who leave comments on YouTube videos are kind and encouraging, the longer you are on the site, the more likely it is you will encounter trolls, those negative people who will give your videos a thumbs-down just because they can and who hide behind fake names in order to leave nasty comments.

While it is tempting to fight back against mean commenters, I have found that the best thing to do is just ignore them. These types of people love to push buttons; they want creators to engage with them in hopes they can escalate the fight.

What do I do when someone leaves an inappropriate comment on one of my videos? I delete the comment and block the person from my channel. I do the same for anyone that leaves inappropriate comments on my other social media accounts, too.

My stance has always been that if I would not allow someone to speak to me a certain way in person, I certainly will not allow them to do it online. Especially when I do not even know who they are.

People online can be mean; they lash out because they themselves are unhappy. As the saying goes, "Hurt people hurt people." And since YouTube allows users to hide behind screen names, it is easy for these types of viewers to leave negative comments.

If you are going to be on YouTube, you will have to develop a thick skin. Keep your focus on creating good content and connecting with the viewers who are kind; the bad ones are not worth your time. And, hey, at least they watched your video, and you earned AdSense from it!

CHAPTER NINE:

A DAY IN THE LIFE

Being a YouTuber involves more than just filming and uploading videos. In this chapter, I will share a day in my life of everything I do to film, edit, upload, and release YouTube videos, including how I film both sit-down and vlog-style content. And remember, I film everything on my iPhone.

First up, I will walk you through the process for uploading videos to my main channel, which is simply named "Ann Eckhart." I currently upload a new video on my main channel three to four times a week, depending on if I have anything actually to film. Since this channel focuses on unboxings and hauls, I have to have something to open to film.

I like to film videos in advance as much as possible. For instance, I filmed a video today that will go up tomorrow. And tomorrow I plan to film two more videos that will go up later in the week. I schedule my videos to go live simultaneously; currently, that means 7 pm Central time. Filming in advance allows me to complete all of the back-end work a day or two ahead of them going live.

To film a sit-down video, I **first arrange my filming space.** I have a table and chair set up in front of some bookcases; the table holds whatever it is I am unboxing. I also have a hospital tray table – the kind on wheels – that holds my phone. Yes, you read that right! No fancy tripod for me as I just prop my phone in its stand onto the table and adjust the height for the best angle. Hey, it works for me!

I gather everything I will need for the video, including whatever I am going to unbox or haul, scissors to open things up, my reading glasses or a magnifying glass to read small print, wet wipes to clean up any messes, lip balm to prevent my lips from drying out, and a bottle of water to keep my mouth hydrated.

Once I have everything in place, and the camera is at the right angle, I press record and start filming. I have been making YouTube videos for over ten years now and can usually film in one take, meaning I do not start and stop talking or filming. Occasionally, I will do a little editing of the footage; but I often only need to cut out the first and last seconds to come up with the final product.

After I have finished filming, I clean up and put everything away. I do this immediately to make way for the next video I will film and not get overwhelmed by the mess!

I then sit down with my iPhone and open **Settings**. Under **Display & Brightness**, I click on **Auto-Lock** and change the time to **Never**. Why? Because I want to make sure my screen does not go into sleep mode, which will stop the upload. This is an important step and one that I am embarrassed to admit that I often forget.

Next, I open the **iMovie app.** The app connects to my camera roll, and from here, I can add the video clip or clips into the app. I watch the video from beginning to end and make any cuts I feel are necessary. I then save the video by simply clicking **Save Video** within the app. iMovie saves the finished video back onto my camera roll.

Once the finished video is saved from iMovie to my camera roll, I **open the YouTube app on my phone,** make sure I am logged into my "Ann Eckhart" channel (remember, I have two channels; fortunately, the YouTube app makes it easy to alternate back and forth between the two with one click), and **click on the + sign inside of the circle** at the bottom of the page to begin the upload process.

I choose to **Upload a video**, which opens up my camera roll. From here, I select the video I just created in iMovie. I make sure that the **privacy setting is turned to "Private"** so that the video does not go live immediately (remember that I schedule my videos in advance; plus, I need to do some work on the back end before going live).

I then click **Upload** and wait for the video to be uploaded to my channel. How long this takes depends on the length of the video as well as the speed of your internet or WIFI connection.

Once the video has successfully been uploaded, I **switch over to my desktop computer to** take care of the back-end details, which is much easier to do on my laptop versus my phone. I log onto YouTube and go into my **YouTube studio**. I then click on the **Content** icon link on the left-hand side of the page and am taken to my channel videos list. The video that I just uploaded should be the very first video at the top of the page. I hover my mouse next to the video, which will reveal several icons. I click on the **pencil icon**, which is called **Details,** to access the **Video details** page.

Once on the video details page, I type in a **keyword-loaded title** so that people who are not subscribed to my channel might find it. I also try to make the title sound exciting to encourage people to watch it. There are so many videos on YouTube these days, making it highly competitive. You must be creative in getting people to click on your videos, especially when they first go live.

After the title, I go into a Word document I have on my computer and copy/paste a block of text that I put into the **description box.** For both of my channels, I link my Amazon store, where I have my books, reselling products, and household favorites listed. I also link my Freebies & Deals Facebook Group, Facebook page, Twitter feed, and Instagram account. I provide an email for business inquires as well as my P.O. Box for viewer mail.

I also include a **Disclaimer**: This is not a sponsored video. If disclosed, some products were sent to me for review. Links may contain affiliates/referrals. The disclaimer is important per FTC rules. At the very bottom of the page is a **Paid Promotion** section where you check a box if you received money for your video. If the video I was uploading had been sponsored, I would have also needed to disclose that in the description box and verbally stated it in the video.

At the bottom of the description box, I add **three hashtags**, which YouTube will put at the top of the video when it goes live. This is a new YouTube feature, and it works to help people find similar videos through hashtags. For instance, if the video is a Halloween-themed Dollar Tree haul, I would use the hashtags *#dollartree #haul* and *#halloween*.

The **Tags** field is at the very bottom of the page. Here is where you can add even more words (think of tags as hashtags without the # symbol) to help potential viewers find your videos when they do a YouTube search. I keep an extensive list of these tag words, separated by commas, in the same Word document that I have my description box information. I can simply copy and paste this block of words into the tags section of every video. Note that the tags I use on my *The Reselling Report* channel are different from those I use on my vlog channel. I then click on the **SAVE** button before moving on to edit another section.

Next, I monetize my video by clicking on the **Monetization icon (the "$" symbol).** Clicking on that dollar icon brings me to the **Video monetization page**. At the top of the page is a **Monetization box**; I select **On** from the drop-down menu. This will then allow me to access the option under the **Type of ads** section of the page. I check every box available to me: **Overlay ads, Sponsored cards, Skippable video ads,** and **Non-skippable video ads.** The **Display ads** option is automatically selected for you by YouTube.

At the bottom of this page is **Location of video ads.** If my video is over 10 minutes long, I can select all three options: **Before video (pre-roll), During video (mid-roll),** and **After video (post-roll).** Under the During video (mid-roll) option, click on **MANAGE MID-ROLLS,** which brings up a pop-up window titled **$ AD BREAKS.** Here is where I can choose where the ads that run in the middle of my videos will appear. These ads bring in the most AdSense revenue, so it is essential to make sure you place them strategically. Too many ads can turn viewers off, but not enough can negatively affect your AdSense earnings. I generally like to place ads around the four-to-five-minute marks of each of my videos, although for really long videos (over thirty minutes), I will use less so as not to turn off viewers with too many ads.

On the **$ Ad breaks page**, you can click on + **AD BREAK** to add in however many ads you want to appear. Let us say that the video I am working on is 20 minutes long. I will likely add in two ad breaks. I will then move over to the **PLACE AUTOMATICALLY** column to enter in the times of six and twelve minutes, or around thereof. Note that you can also manually place the ads using the scrolling template at the bottom of the page, but I personally find it easier to just enter in the times. Once I am done placing my ads, I click on the **CONTINUE** icon to be taken back to the Video monetization page.

After I have typed in my title, copied, and pasted in my description and tags, and set up my video's monetization, I then go back to the main **Video detail page (the pencil icon titled "Details")**. Until now, I have been using the links on the left side of the page to edit my video's information. Now I will focus on the right side of the page and the options that appear there.

I like to schedule my videos, and I do this under the **Visibility** section. When I uploaded my video from my iPhone to YouTube, I made sure that it was set to "Private." Now I can change that from **Private to Unlisted, Members Only, Public (set as instant Premiere)**, or **Schedule**. I click on the **Schedule** option, which brings up a new window of possibilities. I choose to schedule my video for the following day at 7 pm Central time, meaning my video will stay private until YouTube publishes it at that time.

Note that I could also choose the **Set as Premiere** option so that my subscribers would see a live countdown before the video goes live. Premiere also features a live chat option where viewers can chat with one another while the video plays. Some creators schedule premieres to be in the chat once the video goes live to talk with their viewers. Premieres are a great way to encourage engagement with your viewers by providing you a way to connect with them directly. Chatting with your viewers when your videos go live does help increase engagement and create more loyal subscribers, so it is something to consider doing, at least from time to time.

Once I have scheduled my video, I click on **DONE,** and the pop-up window collapses. Note that you do not have to schedule your videos to go up at any particular time; you could just make them live once you have added your title and description along with setting up the video's monetization. However, the YouTube algorithm seems to favor channels where the videos go up on set days at set times. And if you like to film videos ahead of time, scheduling them will help keep you organized. Many YouTube creators will film several videos on the same day and schedule them to go live over the following days or even weeks.

The following section you can attend to is **Playlists.** Playlists allow you to set up categories for your videos. For instance, I have playlists for Ebay videos, subscription boxes, vacation vlogs, and shopping hauls. If you create different types of videos, even if they are under the same general theme, you may want to consider creating playlists. When someone watches a video in a playlist, it will automatically play the next video in the line-up. Therefore, playlists help keep viewers on your channel and watching your videos.

The next section is the **End Screens.** Here you can add **Elements** to the end of your video that viewers can click on. You can add links to the following: **Video, Playlist, Subscribe, Channel, Link,** and **Merchandise.**

Adding a **Video element** lets you choose from **Most recent upload, Best for viewer,** or **Choose specific video.** I typically select the "Best for viewer option," but you can decide what is best for each video. For instance, if you referenced another one of your videos in the video you are uploading, you could select that one.

If you have created **Playlists** on your channel, you can also choose to add one of those to your video. **Subscribe** is another option, and along with "Video," Subscribe is my favorite option to add. **Channel** allows you to add another channel; I use it to promote my own second channel. **Link** lets you add a clickable link to a URL that takes the viewer off of YouTube and to another site. And finally, **Merchandise** will take viewers to items you have created using the TeeSpring design feature that YouTube offers to channels with 10,000 or more subscribers. I have created merchandise using YouTube's TeeSpring feature as well as on the off-site platform TeePublic.

I typically only choose the "Video" and "Subscribe" elements for my videos; getting viewers to watch another video on my channel and having them subscribe are the two most important things I would like them to do. You want to be careful of loading too many end screen elements as your screen will look too cluttered to viewers, and they likely will not choose any of the options available.

The last box you can open is **Cards,** which, according to YouTube, "are designed to complement videos and enhance the viewer experience with relevant info." Cards help to point viewers to your other videos and off-YouTube content. You have four different types of **Cards** to choose from: **Video, Playlist, Channel,** and **Link.**

Video cards allow you to link to another public YouTube video that viewers might be interested in. **Playlist cards** let you connect to another public YouTube playlist. **Channel cards** will enable you to link to a channel that you want to direct viewers to; for example, maybe you are doing a collaboration video with another creator, so you create a "Channel card" to link them directly. And finally, **Link cards** allow you to link to **Associate website cards, Crowdfunding cards,** and **Merchandise cards.**

I personally do not use the "Card" options, feeling that the "End screen" options provide the same benefits. However, as you continue with your YouTube journey, you can take time to play around with the "Card" features to see if they work for you.

My title, description, tags, monetization, schedule, playlist, and end screen options are all finished. I am now ready to tackle the final task before my video is ready to launch: the **thumbnail**. A YouTube thumbnail is the image that appears next to the title of your video. It is the first thing a potential viewer sees, and it is imperative to help get people to click on your video and watch it.

You can use several design apps and programs to create correctly sized YouTube thumbnails. I personally use the **Thumbnail Maker app**, which is available from Apple and on Android devices. YouTube thumbnails need to be 1280x720 pixels; be uploaded in JPG, GIF, or PNG format; and remain under the 2MB limit.

To create my thumbnails, I first select an image. Sometimes I will use a photo, other times graphics, and in some cases, I will use both. I typically take a screenshot from my video and use that, adding text with the app. Using an app such as Thumbnail Maker makes it extremely easy to create my thumbnails right on my phone.

And once I save the finished product, I can add it to my video using the **YouTube studio app** on my phone to upload it directly to my channel.

At that point, my video is complete and ready for YouTube to make it live at the scheduled time!

I also have a vlog channel, *Ann Eckhart Vlogs*, but the process of uploading videos to that channel is relatively the same as it is on my main channel. The only difference is in the filming. While I focus on sit-down videos for my main channel, when I am filming a vlog, I am either filming myself or the events around me but not from a sitting position.

When filming video clips using my phone, I make sure to hold it horizontally, not vertically. Filming on an iPhone held vertically will result in black bars appearing on either side of your footage. Filming horizontally makes it so that your footage takes up the entire screen. When I am vlogging, I simply film my various video clips, which are automatically saved to my phone's camera. When I am ready to put all of the clips together, I do the same as I did for uploading my main channel video using my iPhone:

- I put all the clips together in iMovie
- I save the finished video to my camera roll

- I make sure to turn the sleep mode off on my phone so that my camera will not switch off during the uploading process
- I open the YouTube app and click on the "upload video" + sign in a circle icon at the bottom of the page
- I choose the video from my camera roll
- I click upload
- Once the video is uploaded, I switch over to my computer
- I add in my title, fill out the description box, add in my three leading hashtags, copy/paste my list of tags, monetize the video, choose a playlist, add my end cards, and finally schedule the time and date I want the video to go live

Once my videos go live, I then share them out to my social media accounts. I use the **Share icons** located underneath my videos to post them to my Facebook page, Twitter account, and Pinterest board. I also put up a post on Instagram, both on my page's feed as well as in my "stories." Since I have over 10,000 Instagram followers, I am able to add the "swipe up" feature to my stories, allowing followers to go straight to my video from Instagram.

When I had my blog, I would also post my video there.

And that is it! That is the entire process I go through to film, edit and upload YouTube videos. I am sure that if you have never done it before, it can seem overwhelming. But trust me when I tell you that after you have uploaded a few videos of your own, it will become second nature.

The other work I do in relation to YouTube is answering emails from companies who reach out with sponsorship or product offers. Of course, driving is often a part of my vlog videos, so I need to track my miles and any money I spend on my channel. And since I have a channel dedicated to unboxings and hauls, I have a lot of STUFF that I need to organize; some get gifted, some get resold, but it all takes time to deal with.

I only do YouTube because I love it. It really is fun for me, and it gives me a way to connect with other people, which is hard for me to do as I am a full-time caregiver for my elderly father. I love opening subscription boxes and vlogging while out shopping. The AdSense money, sponsorship dollars, and free products are all great, too, but at the end of the day, if I am not having fun on YouTube, I will not do YouTube.

Do what you love, and the money will follow in life...and on YouTube!

With just a camera and a computer, anyone can start a YouTube channel. However, it takes commitment and perseverance to make MONEY on the site. While there are a handful of people who have gotten rich over the years by making videos, for most people, YouTube offers a bit of extra spending money, perhaps even enough to qualify it as a part-time job. How much you earn is up to you regarding how much time and effort you are willing to put into producing quality content that viewers respond to.

Putting yourself out there in front of thousands and potentially millions of people is a scary proposition. However, if you approach YouTube for your own personal enjoyment and growth before anything else, you will have a successful channel that also brings you some income.

YouTube can be stressful. Dealing with negative comments, having to redo videos, and navigating through technical difficulties can all take their toll. The good thing is that your YouTube channel is YOURS. You can put up as many videos as you want or as few as you want. Need a break? Take it! Step away for a few days, a week, or even a month. Yes, consistency is rewarded on YouTube, but not at the expense of your mental health.

Start your YouTube channel for fun. And at the beginning, just focus on your channel. No need to worry about all of the social media stuff and back-end work. Just get some videos up to get your feet wet. No one likes the first videos they film, and that is okay. Not looking into the camera, realizing you have a stain on your shirt, mispronouncing words....it all comes with the territory.

Practice may not make perfect, but trust me that the more videos you film, the more comfortable you will become. You will find your footing and your voice. Just stick with it, and once you can monetize your content, you will be even more proud of the work you have put in.

With all the work involved, why do I make YouTube videos? Because it is FUN! However, not only do I enjoy creating my videos, but they also earn me money through AdSense and sponsorships plus affiliate and referral links. My videos also drive traffic to my Amazon Author Page, where I sell my books. Sometimes viewers buy the merchandise I have for sale, both from the TeeSpring links that appear under my videos and my TeePublic store, which I link in my description box.

My YouTube channel works in coordination with my books and social media sites to help solidify my brand. My YouTube channels drive traffic to my other sites, and my other sites drive traffic to my YouTube channels. All work together to create the businesses that I run from the comfort of my own home with only myself to answer to. I love being my own boss and owning my time. My freedom is more valuable than any AdSense payout I could ever receive!

ABOUT THE AUTHOR

Ann Eckhart is an author, YouTube creator, and reseller based in Iowa. She has written numerous books about reselling, YouTube, and making money online. She also designs planners, journals, and notebooks under the Jean Lee Publishing pen name.

You can also connect with Ann on the following social media networks:

FACEBOOK: https://www.facebook.com/anneckhart/

TWITTER: https://twitter.com/ann_eckhart

INSTAGRAM: https://www.instagram.com/ann_eckhart/

ANN ECKHART YOUTUBE CHANNEL: https://tinyurl.com/y4tb92dy

ANN ECKHART VLOGS YOUTUBE CHANNEL: https://tinyurl.com/yxjqn6d2

COPYRIGHT

COPYRIGHT 2021

www.ingramcontent.com/pod-product-compliance
Lightning Source LLC
Chambersburg PA
CBHW071251050326
40690CB00011B/2346